SELF-HELP
THROUGH
SELF HYPNOSIS

by James Keenan
with introduction by W.C. McCall, M.D.

BOOKS FOR BETTER LIVING • CHATSWORTH, CALIFORNIA

Acknowledgements

Obviously this book is not based solely on my personal experiences with hypnosis therapy. It is to a great degree a reflection of the combined experiences of many practictioners and researchers of the amazing phenomenon of self-hypnosis. I would like to thank those distinguished men and women collectively here. I am also indebted to W. C. McCall, M.D., not only distinguished himself in the medical community but in the field of hypnosis therapy as well.

I would also like to acknowledge my indebtedness to The Self-Discovery Institute Center for their consent to use direct quotations from a tape recording produced and owned by the Self-Discovery Institute Center.

James Keenan
San Clemente, California

CONTENTS

Introduction

by W. C. McCall, M.D.

Hypnosis occurs in every person every day of his life. A person so engrossed in a TV program, book, or movie that he doesn't hear something said to him, could certainly be said to be in a trance.

Africans, Australian aborigines, and American Indians accomplished healing and other miracles through rhythmic chanting, monotonous drum beats, and catalepsy to "drive the devils out."

I have been interested in hypnosis since 1948, when as an undergraduate, I saw it demonstrated by Dr. Dorcus in a psychology class at the University of California, Los Angeles. As a result, I became concerned with the relationship between hypnosis and the workings of the mind and in turn its effect on the body.

Now a general practitioner in Anaheim, California, I took my first course in hypnosis in 1957 from the American Institute of Hypnosis and promptly began to use it with patients who were interested in hypnosis. Since then, I have treated approximately 1,000 patients per year with hypnotic suggestion, for a variety of symptoms and reasons.

I have repaired fractures and lacerations, delivered babies, promoted healing, and, in one case, removed tonsils under hypno-anesthesia.

I have given papers on hypnosis and hypnotherapy in Oaxaca, Mexico; in Barbados to the Flying Physicians' Association; Vienna, Austria; Madrid, Spain; Munich, Germany; Rio de Janeiro, Brazil; and Johannesburg, South Africa.

The heyday of hypnosis occurred during the last half of the nineteenth century and lasted until the birth of psychoanalysis as practiced by Sigmund Freud, at which time it fell into limbo. It was not resurrected until 1954, when the Mental Health Committee of the American Medical Association reported, after a two-year study, "There are definite and proper uses of hypnosis in medical and dental practice. Hypnosis has a recognized place in the armamentarium of qualified medical and dental personnel."

Their definition of hypnosis is, "A temporary condition of altered attention in a subject which may be induced by another person, and in which a variety of phenomena may appear spontaneously or in response to verbal or other stimuli. These phenomena include alteration in consciousness and memory, increased susceptibility to suggestion, and the production in the subject of responses and ideas unfamiliar to him in his usual state of mind."

Since many illnesses are definitely produced or affected by the mind, such as asthma, colitis, atopic dermatitis, duodenal ulcers, headaches, etc., it appears reasonable many illnesses can be healed by the mind. This has been proven by a succession of "faith healers" from Mary Baker Eddy to Oral Roberts—all made famous by their success in healing.

One of my most impressive hypnosis cases was a Dutch lady, who spoke no English. All communication was through an interpreter. She was unable to keep her eyes open because of a burning pain in both eyes. She was continually running into objects and even the walls in a room. Examined by a number of Dutch ophthalmologists, she was told they could find nothing wrong.

She came to this country to visit her son, who knew of my interest in hypnosis. To me, she revealed, under the hypnotic technique of age regression, that she had seen her father in an act of Pedophilia (exposing himself). She was so upset about this incident, she shut her eyes to wipe the sight of this from her mind. Her father had since died.

I told her under hypnosis, she could now forget this event, since it served no useful purpose. Therefore, she no longer needed to keep her eyes closed; she would have no more pain in her eyes (the supposed reason she kept her eyes closed).

11

She was taken into an examining room where I wiped her eyes with a Q-Tip, telling her I was removing the matter from her eyes, and she would have no more pain or visual discomfort. She was amazed to find she could open her eyes and see normally. The cure has been effective to this date. When she returned to Holland, she wanted to sue the specialists she had seen for malpractice.

Hypnosis can even be a life-saver. One elderly man had two friends die after trans-urethral resections (a relatively simple operation to remove obstruction of the bladder neck enabling the patient to void). Even though he seriously needed the operation, this man refused because he felt he too would die. Ultimately, he had complete blockage of his urine. An emergency operation was performed, completely uneventful. The patient awoke, feeling fine and relieved he was still alive, until his catheter became blocked by a blood clot. He was convinced he was doomed. He turned his face to the wall and refused all nourishment or attempts to obtain his cooperation, saying, "Leave me alone, I'm going to die."

After two days, I was convinced he really was going to die. I hypnotized him and told him, "The surgery has been completely successful. You are healing beautifully and normally. The catheter blockage was a minor incident and is over. You are going to get well very rapidly. When I leave, you will drop off into a deep, natural sleep. You will awaken feeling alert, hungry, and so strong you will get out of bed and cooperate fully with the nurses." The next morning he did just that. He soon left the hospital, hale and hearty. He is well and leading an active life today.

Some feel the personal satisfaction and relaxation derived from prayer is actually a form of self-hypnosis. Certainly, many religions promote a form of hypnosis. When you walk into a church, your attention is immediately drawn to a beautiful altar and cross. The attitude of prayer calls for deep, intense concentration.

Even the Bible may be referring to the hypnotic state when it says, "The Lord caused a deep sleep to fall upon Adam." It is even possible hypnosis is the method by which Jesus carried out the Divine Will.

The ability to be hypnotized is an inherent characteristic of man. When the Bible says, "For false Christs and false prophets shall arise and show signs and wonders to seduce even the chosen people," it suggests to me it is impossible for these false prophets to have divine power. Christ, in his wisdom, knowing the method he was using was also available to human beings, was warning his followers.

One definition of hypnosis is, "Zone of concentration surrounded by areas of inhibition" and this is certainly well demonstrated in our churches.

A story is told about a poor preacher who read a book on hypnosis and decided to try it on his flock. Sunday morning, as he preached his sermon, he held his watch on a long chain and swung it back and forth slowly like a pendulum. When he saw the entire congregation was watching it, he said, "You will place $2.00 in the collection plate."

All hypnosis is self-hypnosis. Even when another person is involved, the phenomena are produced by the subject, not the hypnotist. At first, the skilled hypnotist can guide the subject down the road to a successful trance more easily than the subject can achieve alone. Self-hypnosis is frequently taught in a group. A trance is induced, and specific instructions on how to produce a self-hypnotic trance are given.

The feeling during hypnotic trance can best be compared to the state just before you fall asleep at night; you are not awake, and you are not asleep. You are aware of everything occurring about you, but unless it is out of the ordinary, you pay no attention. Most people wrongly expect to feel that they are in a state of involuntary suspended animation, or off in a deep, dark void. During hypnosis the subject will always know everything that is going on. He will never be under the power or control of the hypnotist. He will do only what he wants to do.

A nonsmoking doctor had a wife who smoked. He disapproved of her habit. He had successfully hypnotized her so many times that all he needed to do was cross his two index fingers, and she would immediately drop off into a somnambulistic trance. One night at a party, when she was in the deepest hypnotic state, he suddenly said, "You will stop smoking. Your cigarettes will taste bad." She awoke from her trance and immediately reached for a cigarette from her purse and lit it. She made a wry face and stubbed the cigarette out. She lit another, with the same results. Then, turning to her neighbor, she asked, "May I please have one of your cigarettes? *My* cigarettes taste bad."

14

Anyone can awaken from a trance at any time, although they don't usually wish to do so until told to by the hypnotist. During the trance they have the ability to control unconscious processes of the body. The subject can control pain, bleeding, and even promote healing. Dentists are well aware that relaxation, the fear of dentistry, and even the flow of saliva can be controlled.

The most rapid results in hetero-hypnosis occur when you bypass the critical factor and get the subject to accept as true something which is not, i.e., one hand is heavier than the other. You are dealing directly with the subconscious mind where the feelings are located. Corrective suggestions can then be placed at the level necessary to remove or block undesirable convictions and emotions.

Numerous books have been written on self-improvement such as *The Power of Positive Thinking, I'm O.K., You're O.K., How to Win Friends and Influence People,* etc., and in my opinion, all utilize some self-hypnosis techniques. Certainly, telling yourself, "Every day in every way, I'm getting better and better" is a device to get the subconscious mind to accept this as a true and permanent suggestion.

Much has been said about the dangers of hypnosis. They prove to be gross exaggerations, the most common being "symptoms are often replaced by worse ones," "people could become psychotic after hypnosis," even "permanent paralysis can occur." When I first became active in medical hypnosis, I asked every doctor who practiced hypnosis if he ever had adverse side effects with hypnosis. I never met one who said, "Yes." I myself,

15

after some 10,000 cases, have never had a patient develop a symptom worse than the one given up.

If you keep in mind that all the reactions produced in hypnosis occur within the subject (and the hypnotist has no power), it can be readily understood why it is extremely unlikely a patient will get rid of one symptom and accept another that makes him more uncomfortable in coping with life than he was before.

Self-hypnosis can be the key to a richer, fuller, more comfortable life. It helps you accept the things you cannot change. It helps you cope with a husband or wife, family, and job. It helps put life in the proper perspective and is the safest, longest acting, most effective tranquilizer known to medicine today.

The instructions in this book are complete. You will know the how and why of every step you take in mastering self-hypnosis. Complete practice schedules are given. Apply yourself to these techniques, and you will surely reap the benefits claimed for them.

Hypnotism stands in the same category as chemistry, physics or mathematics. It is based on definite laws and principles discovered through experiment and research. It has developed into a science, a branch of study dealing with the human brain and human consciousness.

I am pleased that a book on self-hypnosis is being presented at this time as a guide to the layman, and I am more than pleased that Jim Keenan has been selected to author such a work. I think you will find he makes each page come alive with meaning.

Chapter 1

ATTAIN PEACE OF MIND

Self-hypnosis is completely enjoyable and results in the following long-term benefits: It relaxes the nervous system; it overcomes negative mental states such as anxiety, fear, and anger; it calms and quiets the mind; it increases emotional control; and it provides you with direct insight into the nature of yourself.

The need for self-hypnosis—a practical and efficient method of attaining peace of mind—is universal.

At the present time, we can take particular advantage of the rewards of self-hypnosis. We live at an accelerated pace which results in increased mental and emotional anxiety. All of the pressures—money worries, domestic difficulties, problems of health, general insecurity, and the dozens of disappointments and frustrations that must be coped with every day—can be relieved and removed through the practice of self-hypnosis on a daily basis.

The Hypnotic State

Some time in the next twenty-four hours you will experience a condition similar to the *hypnotic state*. You will be asleep. It will be a natural sleep that you have prepared your mind and body for by going through the normal procedures of inducing sleep.

You will probably remove all tight-fitting clothing, bathe, open a window for fresh air during your rest, perhaps snap on your electric blanket for comforting body warmth, turn the lights out, and climb into bed. After reviewing the day's events, a particular worry or concern may demand attention or perhaps you will focus on the happier thoughts of romance and sex. Generally, you will then drift off into sleep.

Sleep is very much like the *hypnotic state*—but not exactly. Everything you do in preparation for a night's sleep is very much like everything you would do to induce self-hypnosis—but not exactly. When you undressed, shut the lights off, put your body down on the familiar mattress, turned on your right or left side for the habitual comfort of a particular position, you were actually *suggesting* sleep to your subconscious mind. All human beings are suggestible, and all subcon-

18

scious minds are subject to suggestion.

Suggestion is the foundation of hypnosis. A conditioned reflex influences our mind and body, producing an exaggerated form of suggestibility. The science of inducing this sleep-like condition is called hypnotism. It is important to repeat that hypnosis is not the same as sleep, although the very word is derived from the name of "Hypnos," the Greek God of sleep. When we sleep, we do not retain our normal reflexes. In the hypnotic state, the reflexes are present, in fact, sharpened. We react more profoundly to suggestion in a hypnotic state.

Another area of comparison is the similarity of the dream state in both a subject under hypnosis and a person asleep. The mind is turned inward, self-absorbed in fantasy, disassociated from the conscious mind, and to varying degrees, withdrawn from reality. While under a hypnotic trance we retain total control and awareness. Not so in simple sleep. Has your mate told you how loud you snore? Were you aware that you snored at all?

We can enter into conversation with the man who talks in his sleep. If we are careful, he will talk just as sanely and often far more frankly than when awake. But when we do awaken him, he remembers nothing of the conversation.

It has been established that a person in a hypnotic state is super alert, susceptible to the influence of other persons, such as the hypnotist, and also highly autosuggestible (he can make suggestions to himself). It is this hypnotic phenomena that enables almost *everyone* to be able to talk himself into or out of anything. The obvious

19

conclusion, therefore, is that through self-hypnosis almost anyone can achieve a richer, more complete life by thinking his fears away.

We can enjoy improved physical and mental health through self-hypnosis. We can actually *talk ourselves into* being more confident, rid ourselves of tension, eliminate that desire for the next cigarette or the next drink, become more self-sufficient, and even direct our bodies toward improved sexual performance.

You can accomplish this by making your subconscious mind work *for* you instead of *against* you. By mastering the techniques of self-hypnosis, the subconscious mind will take over from there. Once you have it working for you instead of against you, you can expect to enjoy an inner peace with yourself, an ability to adjust to any situation that confronts you, experience the joy of accomplishment and the happiness of success.

Does this all sound too mysterious, too far out? Let us assure you that there is nothing mysterious about self-hypnosis. The psychological relationship between the conscious and the subconscious mind is well established in the medical community.

For example, in 1646, Kircher, discovered that drawing a chalk line in front of a bird, particularly a cock, immobilized it completely for a few moments. Later, Heubel managed to make frogs keep still for many hours; he thought of this as similar to inducing sleep.

During the eighteenth century hypnosis came under a spotlight with the findings of Mesmer, who coined the phrase "animal magnetism." J. M. Charcot, at Salpetriere Hospital in France,

20

made an association between hypnosis and neurology, and began treating his patients by suggestion to their subconscious. Later, Pavlov demonstrated hypnotic sleep in animals.

Freud derived from hypnosis his first knowledge of the unconscious, employing those findings in a method of psychoanalysis. Oddly enough, today most psychoanalysis attempts to avoid any trace of suggestion, relying on the confidence established between doctor and patient.

Director of the School For Advanced Studies in France Paul Chauhhard, wrote in the 1950s, "The trickery of sorcerers, the possessed patients, the doctors who induced convulsions and the performances of hypnotists combined to discredit hypnosis—a remarkable phenomenon. Once it had been taken out of the hands of charlatans, hypnosis achieved respectable entry into physiological laboratories."

Beyond Consciousness

It is known that the subconscious cannot reason for itself. It will do whatever the conscious mind tells it to. You control your conscious mind. You must instruct your conscious mind to tell your subconscious mind what it is you expect of it. The instruction to the conscious mind as to what message to relay to the subconscious must be done *before* the self-hypnosis session, because hypnosis, itself, is the method used to bypass the conscious mind, once the session is underway.

How do you bypass the conscious mind? The answer is simple and well documented. As a matter of fact you very likely did it today and didn't realize it. Did you concentrate on any single object? The shine on your coffee cup at lunch? The ceiling light in your office? A brush stroke in the painting on the wall? A design in the floor covering? The candle on the restaurant table at dinner? And then you snapped out of it seconds later, never realizing you had just taken a trip *outside your body, outside your conscious mind.*

Just for an instant you escaped from reality. If you did this, then you were hypnotizing yourself. You were bypassing the conscious mind. Had you known the technique of sending a suggestion to yourself, that is unchanged by the suspended conscious mind, you could have very well taken the first step in achieving an important goal you desire.

It is this technique that we hope to teach you in this book.

First of all, let us get some of the fallacies and misconceptions about hypnosis out of the way.

Question: How can I be sure I'll come out of the hypnotic state when I want to?

Answer: It is terminated at will. No one has ever remained indefinitely in the hypnotic state. There has never been a case where the subject did not return promptly to the waking state.

Question: How can I be sure I can be hypnotized? I don't think I can.

Answer: Unless you are feebleminded, the odds are nine to one you can be hypnotized. And you could not have read this far if you were feebleminded. The best subjects are those people who have a compelling motive for *wanting* to be hypnotized. The first step is to overcome your resistance to hypnosis. This can be difficult because the resistance itself may be subconscious. You must truly *want* to be hypnotized. You must truly *want* to accept suggestions to solve your particular problem. Incidentally, the odds are much higher than nine to one that you hypnotized yourself into the problem in the first place.

Question: How do I know I won't do destructive things under hypnosis? Will I become a slave to anything suggested?

Answer: You will retain absolute power to accept only those suggestions you are willing to carry out. Your own moral principles will govern you throughout, and you will reject all suggestions that you consider improper. You will not stay in any trance you wish to terminate.

Question: Will I be put completely asleep and lose an awareness of my surroundings?

Answer: As mentioned, under hypnosis your awareness will actually *increase.*

What we are going to attempt to teach you is an accepted and proven method of influencing your unconscious. The end result should supply you with a method of voluntary acceptance and application of your own suggestions. Examine the day's events. Wasn't your life influenced, in some minute way, by what you saw, heard, or told yourself today? You were reacting to suggestibility. It is normal, so don't worry about it.

Suggestibility is a prime element in the psychology of human behavior. Television commercials employ the principle of hypnotic influence. If you buy a product as a result of the commercial, you *wanted* to believe the commercial's message. In self-hypnosis, as well, you must *want* to

23

achieve your goals, *want* to enter the hypnotic state, *want* to accept the suggestions you will be giving yourself. Now it is our turn to ask you some questions:

Do you want to make your subconscious mind work for you?

Do you want to be calmer, more relaxed?

Do you want to achieve a fuller, richer life?

Do you want to rid yourself of those morbid fears that haunt you?

Do you want to stop that bad habit? Drinking? Smoking?

Do you want new self-confidence in your every thought and action?

Do you want to improve your love life?

Productive results with self-hypnosis take motivation and practice. Although there are some cases on record that indicate improvement after just one session, the majority of cases require repeated sessions before lasting results are realized.

Your Self-Hypnosis Plan

Now we are going to suggest something to you. Decide now to devote five minutes a day for the next month to your self-hypnosis therapy. You need not be in a deep state of hypnosis to benefit from the session, but it is likely that by the second week of your program you will find yourself relaxing more as you repeat the process. Consequently, you will experience a deeper tranquility and be more susceptible to the suggestions you are giving your subconscious mind. By that time, you will be completely convinced you can indeed hypnotize yourself. Everyone capable of planning such a project can become a good subject. The willingness to plan a five-minute-per-day session proves there is motivation present. All that remains is practice. If you accept the theory that what the mind causes the mind can cure, self-hypnosis has tremendous potentialities.

The mind, when enfeebled by nervousness, can be entirely at the mercy of the unconscious (such as in cases of hysteria) and highly subject to the influences of both suggestion and autosuggestion. When we have surrendered to fear of the sexual instinct, we do not consciously know what we are doing.

Many of the drives we harbor within are kept from our consciousness and may be the origin of mental conflicts and neurosis without ever becoming conscious. Even deeper in the unconscious are these drives that have their origin in our infancy or childhood. Some of these drives are hereditary, or they may have been caused by our surroundings and family influences. Whenever we perform an act without thinking about its necessity, we are surrendering to our unconscious.

Suggestion occurs at a lower level psychologically than a considered reaction. Janet said on this theory, "Doubtless this urgent thought is dangerous, as it can easily be wrong or absurd, but it is very powerful. It is even more powerful than reflective belief, as it has not been modified by the doubts that reflection brings."

Different tests have been tried to classify degrees of suggestibility. Richet asked his subjects to shake hands with him and then told them that they could not open their hands; a susceptible subject felt paralyzed. Willpower can be used both

25

therapeutically and educationally. Imagined diseases, phobias, inferiority complexes, persecution mania, and many others are the result of the wrong type of autosuggestion. Unhealthy suggestions occur often enough in everyday life to play an important part in normal behavior. They can be reversed by healthy suggestions being administered under self-hypnosis.

A healthy suggestion used frequently by hypnotic therapists is, "You can control your mind, you can control your body . . . you can do anything you make up your mind to do. Every day in every way you're getting better and better . . ."

Neurotic Jealousy

A woman visited me in Newport Beach, California, some months ago. Although we talked of many other things, I could see she was deeply troubled by some particular problem she had not mentioned. As she became more comfortable during our conversation, she finally blurted out the details of the dilemma she had been wrestling with on a day-to-day basis for a long time. It was jealousy. I had known her husband for some time and knew he was not the type of man who played around. Oddly enough, she also quickly assured me she had absolutely no grounds to suspect her husband of having an affair or even being in search of one.

"I have these dreams almost every night," she insisted. "In each of them my husband is being unfaithful. It wouldn't be so bad if it ended there, and I was over it when I woke up in the morning. But the dream lingers on throughout the day. I know it's unjustified, and to tell you the truth, I feel stupidly guilty of suspecting him of such things. I know he loves me, and our marriage could be such a wonderful relationship, if I wasn't so damned jealous. Don't you see, I can't help it. The feeling is there, and worse, the dreams are there. I've told him about it.

"He says just the fact I know the problem exists and is unfounded means I will eventually work it out by myself. But I think I need some help coping with it. I just don't understand it."

As the conversation progressed, I learned she had been the "ugly duckling" as a youngster, both at school and at home with her sisters and brothers. Furthermore, she had dropped out of high school in her junior year. The man she eventually married was a college graduate. Most of his previous girlfriends had been college girls majoring in education.

As a mature woman, she was no longer an ugly duckling. She had developed into an attractive woman. I explained to her that all too often the image of ourselves we developed in childhood carries over into our adult life, even though we have changed.

I told her that as a young teen-ager, I, myself, had been small physically, and it developed into quite a complex. Between the ages of fourteen and sixteen I grew almost ten inches and gained fifty pounds. Although my new stature was there for me to see, the image of myself being a small-framed human being still lived with me in my subconscious mind.

At age nineteen, I was reading the sports pages of a newspaper. It carried the physical measurements of the contestants in an upcoming middleweight championship boxing match. I recognized that one of the fighter's measurements were almost identical to my own. In that moment, I fed into my subconscious the reasoning it was not capable of itself. From that day forward I had a new image of myself. My subconscious thought of me as being quite normal in size—maybe even an athlete! The suggestion had been made, and my subconscious took it from there. My complex disappeared.

The woman's real problem was not an unfaithful husband. It was her own insecurity. She pictured herself as unattractive, uneducated, and inferior to her husband's former girlfriends. Her subconscious had developed the habit of thinking of her this way. The subconscious had to be guided in a new, healthier direction. I suggested hypnosis. She took my advice and the hypnosis advanced to self-hypnosis. She later reported it took about six weeks for the dreams to cease. She now sees herself in a new light, with a more valid, positive image of herself. The end result was no more jealousy and a happier and more rewarding marriage.

One could go on and on citing the games our subconscious mind plays with our lives. It must be guided, steered away from those unhealthy, morbid roads it has learned to follow automatically by the introduction of new habits patterns.

Habit Formation

There is an immense variety of acts we ourselves do not consciously control, for instance, the coordination of the brain and the muscles. On another level is the para-conscious. It deals with those activities which were once conscious but now have become a habit, and the performance of which is better if no longer given attention.

This kind of habit formation was demonstrated to me when I was a young reporter on a New York newspaper. I was surprised to see how many of my fellow reporters were "two-fingered maniacs" at their typewriters. They could type as fast as any trained secretary, yet they used only two fingers because they had never been taught the proper method.

One night, during a lull in the flow of copy, I put a group of them to a test. I asked them where certain letters were located on their typewriters. They were all stumped except for one old timer who remembered the "q" was in the upper left-hand corner. He only remembered because the "q" on his machine had been broken for months, and he had to write that letter in when typing. But put their fingers on the keyboard, and their subconsciouses knew exactly where each letter was. It could be they learned to type *while concentrating deeply* on another subject, and their subconsciouses had consumed the keyboard through repeated suggestions until they formed a habit. They now typed better when they didn't consciously think about it.

An example of how unhealthy habit formation works in the subconscious mind can be observed in the case of the five-year-old little girl who had suffered a form of epileptic seizures from the time of her birth. At age two, medication was prescribed that almost halted the seizures entirely. The medication, unfortunately, contained a high potency barbituate.

29

The doctors were forced to take the little girl off the drug at age four, and the seizures returned. After a year of almost daily seizures, the physicians decided it was time to return to the drug, despite the dangers involved. When the mother asked why, they explained that the little girl's subconscious mind might become used to the idea that there was *supposed to be* a seizure every so often, and would induce the seizure on its own as a matter of habit.

Habit is the key word. The subconscious mind reacts to repetition. That fear you might be harboring didn't occur to your subconscious mind just once. It was repeated, and now may be deepseated. The taste of that cigarette was repeated. The calm after that alcoholic drink was repeated. The subconscious mind becomes used to the feeling, the sensation—even the agony.

Now we are saying to you, teach your subconscious mind a new habit. A healthier habit. And repeat it.

Repeat it five minutes a day. Along about the tenth or eleventh day your subconscious mind will accept the suggestion completely, and you will have acquired a new habit. But this time it will be a habit that counteracts the subconscious mind's previous self-destructive habit, whether it was cigarette addiction or the input of irrational fears, etc.

Your automobile is probably an important part of your life. Your automobile and the self-hypnosis process are somewhat alike. You feed gasoline into your car, the same as you feed a problem into your conscious mind. You turn the key and the engine starts, the same as positive suggestion and relaxation move your subconscious mind into action.

The subconscious mind *wants* to do what is good for you. You must tell it what you want it to do for you, and it will automatically carry it out.

Your automobile will take you where you want to go. If you drive it up on the curb or into a lamp post, it automatically follows instructions. Your subconscious mind just as easily will be guided into the need for a cigarette, the desire for alcohol, the fear of this or that, or the idea that you will not perform adequately in the sex act, if you instruct it to do so.

What we are going to try to teach you is the method by which you can guide or steer your subconscious mind straight down the proper lane of traffic, with no fender bending, or mind-bending, for that matter, along the way.

Now it is time for you to do a self-analysis, and thus plan just how self-hypnosis is going to be employed to help rid yourself of your problem. Ask yourself these questions:

What habit do I want to break? Am I overweight? Do I drink too much? Do I smoke too much? Do I suffer from nervous tension? Do I get tired for no reason at all? How long does it take to go to sleep at night? Am I a good sex partner? Am I often depressed? Do I have a good sense of humor? Is there too much hate in my make-up? Am I selfish? Am I jealous?

Do I like myself? Do I enjoy my life? Do I get along with people easily? Am I afraid of crowds? Heights? Small places? Am I lonely? Can I give and accept love? Am I shy? Do I fear leaving the house, going out in the world? Do little, unimportant things disturb me? Am I a hypochondriac? What am I going to accomplish today? Has a lifetime of worry claimed me?

Chapter 2

REDIRECT YOUR ATTENTION

Self-hypnosis must be practiced. All the talking, studying, or thinking about it you do will produce no results. Theorizing is worth absolutely nothing in this study. You must practice self-hypnosis and know it by experience. In effect, you must develop a *working relationship* with your unconscious mind.

Self-hypnosis is simple, delightful, and extremely rewarding in terms of tranquility, balance, and clarity of mind. You will verify these claims if you apply yourself sincerely to the techniques taught in this book.

We are hypnotized by movement. We are hypnotized by activity. We are hypnotized by our desires and by the objects of our desires and by a multitude of illusory ideas and notions. Actually ten thousand things in our life lure us toward the hypnotic state.

So long as you are carried along helplessly by the movement and subsequent illusions of your everyday thinking, you can never know who you really are, nor can you ever experience life as it really is. Reality, or the true nature of the world, is often distorted as it filters through the uncontrolled movements of the mechanical mind.

As you cannot see through turbulent water, so can you not see through the movements of your chaotic mind. But once the movement is stilled, you will experience your original nature, learning who you are and what it is you want to accomplish.

Experiment In Concentration

It is important to be able to concentrate your attention upon one point before you can practice self-hypnosis.

We are now going to attempt an experiment in concentration. This is not in effect self-hypnosis, but it will prepare you and develop your ability to concentrate. Following these instructions, practice this experiment every day for the next five days.

The room must be dark.

Sit in a comfortable chair, and loosen all tight fitting clothing.

Place a lighted candle about an arms length in front of you. Try to avoid any draft on the candle flame which would make it waver. It is best if the flame rises straight and steady. Now gaze fixedly at the candle flame. Blink normally, but keep your attention upon the flame. Do not look away from the flame even for a split second. Try not to allow your mind to wander.

Concentrate in this manner for three minutes. Your estimate of time will be sufficient and will become extremely accurate as the days progress.

Now close your eyes.

Looking into the darkness of your closed eyelids, you will see the afterimage of the candle flame. The purpose of this exercise is to keep that afterimage in sight as long as you possibly can and to keep it steady in the center of your vision. Try not to let it waver or move about. If the afterimage recedes or fades out of sight, attempt to bring it back into view, all this with your eyes closed.

Continue this second part of the concentration experiment for three minutes, the same length of time you originally gazed at the actual flame. This technique will train your mind not to wander, to obey you, and to hold itself on one point, a skill that will serve you well when later practicing self-hypnosis.

The Freudian Complex

We mentioned how vulnerable we are to the pressures of life and our surroundings in twentieth century American society. Many psychologists make a flat statement that basic to every case of mental disease is the Freudian complex. In reality, the Freudian complex is a posthypnotic suggestion, as we earlier explained. This type of posthypnotic suggestion differs from what we see in a hypnosis demonstration.

The hypnotist is careful that suggestions do not arouse conflict or antagonism in his subject. In the Freudian complex, the repression occurs *because of* conflict and now acts with all the compulsive force of a posthypnotic suggestion, causing further conflict. This is known as unconscious motivation, a concept basic to any study of mental disease.

The Freudian complex is imposed by life itself and is not under our direct control. A situation that happened in our childhood can be *burned in* for twenty, thirty, forty years, or more. A therapeutic hypnotist can guarantee to remove his posthypnotic suggestion at a minute's notice, no harm done. Such a guarantee cannot be made in the case of the Freudian complex, even though it is a special form of posthypnotic suggestion that we imposed upon ourselves earlier in life. This characteristic of the Freudian complex causes the personality to do curious things, to think curious things, to dream curious things. Each of us has to face reality, so to build up certain mechanisms to reduce the pain of the particular conflict, we disguise it in order to live a normal life.

The best way to void a posthypnotic suggestion of its compulsive power is to bring it into consciousness. This puts an end to the process of unconscious motivation, and the posthypnotic suggestion is now part of our normal conscious life.

It is important to remember the complex we are talking about is based on an unpleasant experience which was thrown out of consciousness into the unconscious years before. The conscious mind not only refuses to remember this original experience, but has built up a whole set of defense mechanisms to make sure it stays where the conscious mind wants it, namely, in the unconscious mind, while the patient pursues a normal life and happily ignores the complex in question. These defense mechanisms, when reinforced by time, become so strong they repel every attempt to get at them.

Uncovering The Truth

I once was involved in the investigation of a murder case in which a man was being tried for the slaying of his wife and her lover. The legal evidence against the defendant was overwhelming and seemed to prove beyond a shadow of a doubt that he did in reality shoot both his wife and her paramour while they were in bed together in what must have been a very passionate love scene.

Prosecuting the case, however, became more difficult than expected because the defendant's alibi appeared to be ironclad. When questioned by the district attorney's office, by the grand jury, and even while being questioned by his own attorney during his lengthy trial, the defendant never wavered, never made a mistake in his facts, and more important, convinced everyone he was telling the truth. He testified he was nowhere near the bedroom on the night of the murders. His alibi story, repeated time and time again, was letter perfect. It was obvious to everyone he himself believed it thoroughly. His lawyer went so far as to confide to me, "If he is guilty, the memory of murdering his wife and his best friend while they were in bed is so horrible he has blotted it out completely." That is exactly what had happened.

During his incarceration, as the trial progressed, a strange thing developed. The defendant exhibited extreme fear at being in closed-in quarters. At first this emotional disturbance was credited to the fact he was in jail, living in a small cell, and couldn't cope with this type of punishment.

Further investigation into his background revealed that during World War II he had passed all psychological tests and was accepted into submarine duty. Nothing could be more confining than that. How could a man who had lived for months in the confines of a small submarine a hundred feet below the surface of the ocean suddenly be inflicted with claustrophobia?

What happened in this case was the sight of his beloved wife engaged in an act of infidelity was so horrible to his conscious mind the defense mechanisms we mentioned earlier had disguised the entire scene for him. But the posthypnotic suggestion that came out of the entire ugly affair remained in his unconscious mind. He found himself hiding in a small closet with the door closed, listening to the sounds of sex coming from his bedroom. It must of been an extremely painful experience for him; the only memory of it that remained was the uncomfortable confinement of that tiny closet. Thus, a fear was born—not a fear or hatred of women, but a fear of small enclosed places.

Where does hypnotism fit into this general picture? First, it is of prime importance as an uncovering technique. In hypnotism we can use what we call regression. Under regression, an individual can relive his life in his memories, sometimes years later.

Thus, with the use of hypnotism we can often uncover the original experience which led to the complex, to the posthypnotic suggestion responsible for the mental symptoms. It has been estimated that fifty to sixty percent of all people can be hypnotized to a depth where such recall is possible.

Uncovering the original destructive experience is only step one. The individual, through his defense mechanisms, has built up an entire life pattern in which this complex has played a vital part. It would be foolish to think that we can correct this pattern in one, two, or three hypnosis sessions. We must begin a sustained attack on the symptoms themselves.

But a note of caution here. The removal of the symptoms in a mental disorder is similar to removing a knife from a wound and leaving the cut open and bleeding. Infection may remain, and new symptoms will probably develop. For example, it has been established that it is relatively easy to cure heavy drinking by means of a hypnotic suggestion. However, most doctors will agree that heavy drinking is a symptom of a mental disorder. The real cause has not been touched. The heavy drinker will often replace this symptom with another symptom, perhaps drugs which is worse than the first. Conclusion: getting at the symptom is not enough—we must get to the cause. In effect we must try to outflank, outmaneuver, and outsmart the defense mechanisms and direct the personality up a new path.

Granted, we have used a dramatic example—a murder case—to demonstrate the importance of autoanalysis. It is probable a murder is not involved in the particular problem you desire to treat through self-hypnosis. We apologize for the dramatics, but the story is true, and it does illustrate one of the secret corners of the human mind. The better we understand these secret corners, the more successful will be our approach to self-help through self-hypnosis.

Like the word discipline, the word concentration seems to denote something unpleasant to the average person. Upon hearing these two words one usually thinks of a great strain, involving a tremendous effort of the will and mental faculties.

Self-hypnosis can and should be an utterly enjoyable form of mental exercise from the outset. You will be disciplining what has been in nearly all cases a badly spoiled mind, and instead of feeling any strain or effort, you will experience the joy of self-improvement and the release from unnatural tension. Thus, we see the true nature of self-discipline—it is one of the highest pleasures and leads to the highest good. You will experience a fascinating exploration into yourself.

If you have practiced the candle concentration technique suggested, you notice a certain relief of tension throughout your body during this particular exercise. This is just the beginning.

In the initial stages of hypnosis, a person learns to concentrate by focusing on a particular object. The object chosen from the external world, might be a candle, a religious image, a work of art, a tree, or a spectacular vista. The object can also be internal, created in the mind, for example, a white dot in the center of your forehead.

Hypnosis practiced without an object is a higher, purer form of hypnosis. Indeed, concentration on an object can be considered preparation for pure and nonobjective hypnosis. It is the reason you were instructed to close your eyes after three minutes and retain the image of the candle in your mind's eye. It will make it easier to picture and concentrate on an imagined white dot in the center of your forehead when we practice the actual self-hypnosis technique.

Guilt And How It Works

I do not want to move away from the subject of hypnotic regression and the importance of autoanalysis without mentioning an interesting story I like to call "the case of the man who loved to walk."

Andy was a married man, and to all outer appearances, completely happy with his home life. He was a good provider and a hard worker. He had no hobbies, with one exception; he thoroughly enjoyed taking a long walk through the streets of Manhattan one or two nights a week, instead of going home for his evening meal. Andy absorbed the fascinating people, the fast pace, and city lights as he strolled down Broadway, Fifth Avenue, or Eighth Avenue—all the way from 59th Street to perhaps 24th Street. The man could certainly walk.

But there is another angle to Andy's story. New York is a city of opportunity. It was a rare night when Andy would make his long walk without being joined by a member of the opposite sex, somewhere along the way. By the time he got to 34th Street it would most often be the age old question of "Your place or mine?" In reality, it was this adventure Andy was searching for on his nights out. He could return home to his wife and children at ten or eleven o'clock feeling refreshed and satisfied. But deep down in his unconscious mind was another feeling—guilt.

It so happens Andy was blessed with a religious mother, who instilled in him during his childhood an exaggerated set of moral values regarding sex.

During his adolescence, he had certain sexual desires he was ashamed of because of his mother's teachings and strict guidelines. The guilt complex was fixed in his unconscious mind as a boy, and it took the ride along with him into adulthood. Once married, Andy replaced the image of his mother with his wife's. To his conscious mind these night walks through the city were really the only outlet he had for his pent-up emotions. He was very happy he could walk for miles and never tire.

And then a strange thing happened. One day on his lunch hour, he was walking by himself down a street near his office. Suddenly he felt a numbness throughout both his legs. Within ten steps he found he could no longer put one foot in front of the other. He was paralyzed. In that single minute, his mind and his body became gripped in hysteria and fear. The word heart attack and stroke loomed in his frantic brain. Holding on to a railing he half dragged himself along the street, hoping to get back to his office. Luckily, a cruising cab stopped, picked him up, and took him home. He still could not move his legs. He remained in bed for almost a week during which time he was examined by two doctors.

Think what had happened to this man. He could no longer walk—the one thing in his life that he valued so much. More startling, the doctors could find nothing physically wrong with his legs or nervous system. It was almost three months later before Andy got around to psychoanalysis and finally hypnosis.

Under hypnosis Andy was regressed to his childhood. The answer was reasonably simple. The guilt about sex and the eventual infidelity to his wife, resulting from these long walks at night, had finally struck back at Andy, creeping out of the unconscious mind and hitting his world of reality with devastating impact. Andy had to face the real cause of his temporary paralysis; he had a deep desire to punish himself because of his guilt. It took six sessions with an accomplished hypnotist and two months of self-hypnosis before Andy was able to walk normally again.

A Los Angeles doctor involved in research of the smoking habit recently published an article in which he said, "The heavy smoker who is trying to quit but can't might try to remember what it was that started him smoking cigarettes in the first place." Can the average person actually recall the circumstances of that first cigarette? Try it. I doubt if you can. Under hypnosis, with regression technique, you probably can—and will!

Self-analysis refers to analyzing and understanding yourself while in a self-induced hypnotic state. We will not attempt self-hypnosis at this stage, but to give you a clue of what to prepare for, think back over your life; what incidents happened to you years ago, incidents that you didn't think were important until perhaps now. But remember you are not in a hypnotic state. You are not engrossed in self-hypnosis as yet. Thus, you may not remember the actual event that caused your problem. But one thing is certain—you are already rehearsing the techniques you will put to extraordinary use once you have fully learned the technique of self-hypnosis.

Withdrawal

I have often heard hypnosis described as a system of withdrawal. It's a good definition.

Withdrawal is the temporary divorce of yourself from the objects of the world around you which continually demand your attention. There is a time to cater to the world around you and to the demands of your senses; there is also a time to put these things aside and proceed systematically with your inner journey toward the discovery of your real, intrinsic self. Remember, the truth is within you. There comes a time when you stop giving a spoiled child the attention he is demanding. It is the same with the outside world. Once a day say to it, "You have had sufficient dominion over me for now." Once a day, at least, you must assert your independence from all that is happening out there. This will become known to you as your five minutes a day of withdrawal, your five minutes a day with self-hypnosis.

You can feel justified in withdrawing temporarily. As a matter of fact, it is your duty to yourself and to your sanity. By so doing, you can return refreshed to the everyday world and your responsibilities.

Now you would not have read this far if there was not something you wanted self-hypnosis to do for you. Think very hard about this subject. It is the most important question you will be asking yourself. Are you sure that you have a clear understanding of just what you want to accomplish by self-hypnosis? You must thoroughly understand the problem at the conscious level in order to have a deeper understanding of the subconscious, non-reasoning level. If you think you have the answer, write it down. Then write it again, rewording it. You should find that already you are beginning to better understand yourself and your problem. This conscious understanding of the problem could be a great assist when you find yourself placed in a self-induced hypnotic state later on.

Now let's review. Just how far have we advanced? We have a better working relationship with our subconscious mind. At least we understand it's there, and we have started to deal with it. We have had a rehearsal in the technique of concentration. Were you able to see the candle's light after you closed your eyes? For how long? If not for the full three minutes—try again. We have also experienced an informal experiment in self-analysis. Are you satisfied with your conclusions? We have asked ourselves, "What is it I wish to gain through self-hypnosis?" Do you have that goal solidly entrenched in your *conscious* mind?

We have determined to devote at least five minutes per day to self-improvement through self-hypnosis. We have learned that complete relaxation of both mind and body is of prime importance to successful self-hypnosis.

The human mind is totally free. Although this freedom presupposes total exercise of reason, we also possess, of course, very powerful drives. Freud, who discovered the unconscious, said, "Psychic processes themselves are of their nature unconscious, and the conscious understanding of them is analogous to the perception of the external world by the sense organs." Many thoughts and actions are not based on reason, but merely transmit instincts and drives from the most profound depths of our being. We can believe something both on rational evidence and by intuitions from our subconscious minds; this latter influence is in fact autosuggestion.

Suggestion appeals to the unconscious mind, not to the reasoning mind.

Chapter 3

RECOGNIZE YOUR PROBLEMS

Let us talk about *hysteria*. It is a word that none of us are willing to accept when applied to ourselves. Perhaps it's because we do not completely understand the medical definition of hysteria.

The hysterical individual is a grown up five-year-old. We can explain it further using the pleasure principle. The hysteric has an intense longing for attention and sympathy. He does not realize that the way to get this attention is by hard work or real accomplishment. As a child he learned he could become the center of attention by throwing a tantrum on the floor and kicking and screaming. This worked so well that as an adult he does the same thing, and we say he is having an attack of convulsions.

There are all kinds of hysterical symptoms besides convulsions—attacks of weeping, paralysis of an arm or a leg, even blindness or deafness. The patient finds it is pleasant to be the center of attention. This knowledge conditions the brain; each time he repeats the hysterical attack, that line of conduct becomes more deeply burned into the brain's memory. He repeats it as often as possible because of the pleasure involved. It becomes a vicious cycle.

Even the hysteric lives in a real world. He does not retreat from reality; rather, he manipulates reality. He still lives with his family, but he uses all his tricks to make its members his slaves. He learns that the best device with which to center attention on himself is to be sick, hence the endless pains, convulsions, indigestion, heart attacks. The hysteric dominates his own private world.

With this explanation of hysteria, is it any wonder that none of us wishes to admit to the "personality crime" it suggests? Fortunately, this type of person is usually easily hypnotized, since many forms of hysteria are caused by suggestion. The subject has spent all his life pursuing the pleasure principle. He is an hysteric by choice, not by compulsion. The choice may be one of the unconscious mind, and the patient may deny indignantly that he wishes to be sick, but psychology now understands that the unconscious mind is as important as the conscious, at least in this matter of mental health.

Thus, the hysteric actively resists cure, but at the same time wants to be cured, odd as that may sound. Consciously he insists he will cooperate in any line of treatment, however, he is delighted to find that it doesn't work. He, of all people, enjoys being sick. He uses his symptoms for three purposes: to get attention; to retreat from reality; and to dominate his family, his friends, and his surroundings.

But, it is an established fact that he is very suggestible, and hypnotism in many cases can produce a cure.

This gets us into the area of the posthypnotic suggestion. What we are suggesting is simply this: it should be pointed out to the patient the extreme pleasure he will get from being well and healthy, the pleasure it will give his family, and above all the added pleasure he will gain through the admiration of his friends and associates. By the sheer force of suggestion, we are able to direct the pleasure principle on to new paths.

More important, you can direct yourself on to these new and rewarding paths. We by no means intend to classifiy everyone under the heading of "hysteric." But everyone may be subjected to mild forms of it.

The need to smoke that next cigarette could be classified as a form of hysteria.

The desire for that next alcoholic drink could be classified as a form of hysteria.

An inferiority complex about one's appearance could be classified as a form of hysteria.

The lack of organization in regard to one's daily routine could be classified as a form of hysteria.

Stage fright, or the loss of confidence when speaking before a large or small audience could be classified as a form of hysteria.

Speech Defects

Stuttering and speech disorders can, in some cases, be classified as a form of hysteria. In Europe, hypnotism is a recognized means of attacking speech defects, though not a sure cure. Those hypnotherapists who have tried to handle cases of stammering know how extremely resistant to treatment this condition may be. It is curious to note that the stammerer is generally a fairly good hypnotic subject. In addition, he will usually talk without any difficulty once he is in the hypnotic state. Some cases of speech disorders are absolutely incurable. On the other hand, a remarkable number of cases can be corrected through hypnosis—and more importantly—through self-hypnosis.

N.V. Kline, a noted psychologist at Long Island University, has reported that hypnotism can be a great help in healing many skin conditions. He mentions an example of a person with a case of psoriasis, a troublesome, chronic skin disease. The disease had proved itself resistent to all forms of treatment over a twenty-year period, yet it cleared up completely under hypnotherapy.

The approach to problems of heavy drinking and excessive smoking is based on that curious control which hypnotism gives us over the autonomic nervous system, and through it, the organs of the body. We suggest that the subject in the future will be deathly sick to his stomach every time he touches alcohol; the taste will be bad; and he will vomit. We may have to repeat the hypnosis session several times, but with a good subject we will probably succeed. Once we get this posthypnotic suggestion working, it is only a matter of time. The unconscious mind will do the rest. We can assure you if alcohol is your problem, you will not get much pleasure from liquor if the very smell of it makes you vomit. You will not be able to even keep it on your stomach long enough to become intoxicated.

Alcoholism is a symptom of a problem personality. The person cannot face reality and chooses the relaxation supplied by liquor as a way out, an escape. We must strengthen the personality. It is important to do everything in our power to make the subject face reality and to supply an escape which meets with social approval. So now is the time to ask yourself, if you are a heavy drinker, with what would I like to replace alcohol?

Relaxing hobbies can be used to take the place of alcohol. Think hard and seriously about a substitute. Later on, you might very well give yourself a posthypnotic suggestion directed towards that hobby. You may decide to devote more time to painting, chess, sports, growing plants, even chasing women or men, as the case may be.

A qualified hypnotist will never take the cure of the heavy drinker for granted. In the back of the alcoholic's mind there will always be the longing for some substitute that will take the place of liquor. Alcoholism is merely a symptom, a signal of more serious trouble.

Hypnotism seems to lend itself to the treatment

of excessive smoking by much the same technique as that used to combat alcohol. In the case of the excessive smoker, however, the condition is not as serious and the treatment simpler.

In our society everyone should try to analyze problems intelligently, to be fully responsible and only accept positive autosuggestions. Everyone should think of himself as an individual. We should try to be optimistic at all times. Man is free to choose his own path. The path you choose for yourself now should be a happy and rewarding path.

Ask yourself, are you one of those people who knows his responsibility to himself but completely ignores it? Or are you going to triumph in your battle with your problem? To quote a politician of recent years—"Why not victory!".

In self-hypnosis, you are involved in the remodeling of your will to improve yourself.

In the past your unconscious was influenced by negative hypnotic suggestion. Now you are going to use self-hypnosis to free yourself.

In this chapter, we have grazed the surface of problems dealing with negative autosuggestion like hysteria, speech defects, heavy drinking, and excessive smoking. In future chapters, we will delve deeper into these problems and the techniques employed to solve them.

Chapter 4

RELAX YOUR WAY TO HAPPINESS

You have been given a substantial background in the theory of self-hypnosis. It is now time for your first lesson in the actual experience of it.

In hypnotic suggestion, the attitude is tremendously significant. Your voice should express conviction. Any effective salesman or public speaker knows that a confident attitude is necessary to bring his audience around to his way of thinking. If suggestions are made in a forceful manner, the order will be obeyed. This is what you must learn to do in directing yourself while under self-hypnosis. Command yourself.

Easy Relaxation Technique

We'll begin with the relaxation segment of the hypnosis technique. The best time for this exercise is right after waking up in the morning.

1. Turn on some music you find pleasing and relaxing. We would suggest that you avoid the use of a radio, if possible. Commercials may interrupt your train of thought. A stereo album of your favorite instrumental would be advisable.

2. Now lower the lights so that there is just a dim light in the room.

3. Recline on a comfortable bed or couch. Make sure your head is elevated slightly by a soft pillow.

4. Loosen all tight-fitting clothing.

5. Now just relax there for a full minute enjoying the music.

6. Say to yourself,

"I am completely relaxed, completely comfortable." Start talking to yourself as though you are another person. Talk to yourself very slowly, but with conviction.

"You will actually feel the sensation of your mind relaxing . . . your body relaxing . . . I want you to imagine your mind drifting down into the soft velvety darkness (at this point close your eyes) going way down . . . all the *way* down . . . all the way down into velvety darkness . . . way down. Actually feel the sensation of your mind relaxing . . . *melting* as it sinks down . . . way down . . . into the soft velvety darkness . . . going way down. It is floating down like a feather . . . floating down into the darkness . . . imagine it floating down . . . going way down. Your eyelids are heavy, and you are sleepy, your mind is sleepy, your body is sleepy.

"Actually feel the sensation of your chest melting, relaxing, every nerve, every muscle in your chest relaxing, melting. Feel the sensation of the muscles in your stomach melting . . . melting away . . . relaxing . . . as your mind sinks deeper . . . and deeper . . . and deeper asleep. Deeper . . . and deeper relaxed.

"I want you to concentrate now on your thighs. They are melting away, relaxing. The large muscles of your thighs . . . picture them melting, relaxing, I want you to concentrate now on your calves and your legs . . . they are melting away, relaxing, hanging loose. As you go deeper, and deeper . . . and deeper asleep. Deeper . . . and deeper relaxed. Now you will picture your feet and you will see the flesh melting off the bone of your feet, relaxing, and melting, as you go deeper . . . and deeper relaxed . . . deeper . . . and deeper asleep.

"I want you to concentrate now on the back of your neck. Untie that knot back there; let it go loose . . . looser . . . looser . . . relaxed . . . melting away. Your mind is going deeper . . . and deeper . . . into the soft velvety darkness. I want you to concentrate now on your arms and your hands, picture the flesh melting off the bone, relaxing, melting, as your mind goes deeper . . . and deeper asleep, deeper, and deeper, and deeper . . . and deeper relaxed.

"I'm going to count from ten down to one. As I count, step by step, you will make your mind, your body, your chest, your stomach, your thighs, your legs, your back, your arms, your hands, relaxed more, deeper asleep until by the time I reach the count of one, you will take a very deep breath, blow it all the way out, and go completely, deeply, asleep.

"Ten . . . your mind is relaxing, melting, sinking into the deep dark velvety darkness, going all the way down.

"Nine . . . your chest is relaxing, melting.

"Eight . . . the muscles in your stomach are relaxing, melting.

"Seven . . . your thighs are melting, melting away . . . relaxing.

"Six . . . your calves are melting away, the flesh from the bone, relaxing, hanging loose.

"Five . . . your entire body is completely relaxed now like a set of clothes hanging over a chair, loosely . . . relaxed . . .

"Four . . . as your mind goes deeper, deeper, deeper asleep.

"Three . . . your entire body is in a state of limbo hanging relaxed.

"Two . . . every nerve and muscle in your body is relaxed and hanging, and your mind is still going deeper, and deeper into the soft velvety darkness.

"One . . . take that very deep breath . . . blow it all the way out . . . and now you are completely, deeply, relaxed.

"I want you to concentrate now . . . and actually *see* that candle flame that you saw before. This time you will see it in your mind's eye. See it. Concentrate on it. It is vivid in your mind's eye—in the center of your forehead. See it. Concentrate on it. Look deeper into it. Nothing but the flame. As you go deeper, deeper . . . and deeper asleep. Deeper, deeper . . . and deeper asleep relaxed. Your mind will concentrate now on nothing but the candle flame that you see in the center of your forehead. Concentrate on it. See it.

"Actually feel the sensation of your mind floating out towards that flame. Floating out towards it.

"Very, very comfortable, very, very relaxed. I want you to awaken now on the count of three feeling very comfortable, normal, free from pain or body discomfort in every way. One . . . getting brighter. Your mind is getting brighter. Three . . . and you're awake!"

Autorelaxation is the most important part of successful self-hypnosis.

You have just experienced the first step in the technique of self-hypnosis. This exercise must be repeated *every* day. Read and re-read this passage on autorelaxation until you have committed it to memory. If you own a tape recorder, you may wish to record the self-hypnosis suggestions, beginning with this one. Inexpensive cassette recorders are available for about thirty dollars. However, if you do not have one, you are in no way handicapped; these exercises can very easily and happily be performed without one.

Chapter 5

YOU ARE THE MASTER

We are indoctrinated to look to the mind as the great solver of problems and our most competent guide through life. We also tend to be awed by the so-called great achievements of the logical intellect. Once you know its true nature, it becomes plain that the mind does not deserve such adulation.

The everyday mind—conscious and subconscious—is a machine.

Yes, the mind is a machine, a mechanism and nothing more. That which gives us the impression of being the source of intelligence, consciousness, and insight is a mechanical apparatus, a super-computer, and a data collector.

This machine is very much like a robot that, because it functions so well, has come to think of itself as a qualified self-governing entity. The mind is like a servant who has taken over super-vision of his master's household. He has so con-vinced the master that he, and he alone, knows what's best, the master, in relinquishing his origi-nal authority little by little, has forgotten that the servant—in this case the mind—has served in any other capacity.

You are the master. Your mind is your servant and tool. Yet you have come to be dependent on its ways, opinions, caprices, conclusions, and theories. This servant which takes over the house-hold of the master lives and is obsessed by one principle: self-preservation. The mind knows once the master awakens to the true situation and re-assumes his original authority, its power is gone. The mind is alert every second of the day and night to make certain this never happens.

The everyday mind, this so-called rational, in-tellectual mind, is untrustworthy so long as it usurps the position of master.

All its guidance, advice, leadership, and prob-lem solving is aimed at producing more problems to be solved. Its trick is always to have problems (you are under the impression they are your problems). The solutions are always soon to be arrived at or later to be arrived at, as long as you adhere to the logical and reasonable plan your mind has arranged as the right path for you to follow.

We spend years coping with and solving problems that didn't exist or never were problems to begin with.

If you will observe the thoughts that come and go in your conscious mind throughout the day, you will note the useless, wasteful, and to a considerable extent, trashy nature of them. Daydreams are nearly always absurd and out of touch with reality. You keep up a running dialogue with yourself that serves no purpose, except to waste precious minutes and hours of your life.

Your mind lusts after what it cannot have or what it is not prepared to go about getting. It gossips, comes to wrong conclusions, and much of the time, engages in thoughts that are unworthy of a human being whose spark of life is burning to its end. Your mind, in its uncontrolled, wayward flight, does everything from cajoling, flattering, and puffing up a false ego in you to crushing you with unnecessary, baseless guilt and self-recrimination. It will sink to any depth of degradation to keep itself and you from realizing for a moment that it has not the vaguest connection with reality. Everything is censored and distorted by our minds.

You are not your mind. Your mind is not you. Your mind is no more you than your arm or head is. It is a wonderful, vital part of you but of no greater importance than any other organ in your body. From early childhood, this mental apparatus has contrived to make us identify ourselves with it.

Your mind does not necessarily know what is best for you. It would have you believe that it alone is best equipped to give you the proper advice in all situations. In truth it is not at all an efficient and dependable guide. Is it giving you the best and proper advice when it tells you you need that next cigarette, that next drink, that you are something less than an equal in society or among your friends, that you are physically unattractive, that you are inefficient, that you are and should be nervous, excited or even fatigued without reason?

The function of self-hypnosis is to control this runaway mind. By so doing, you will see it for what it is, and you will verify the foregoing statements regarding it. When you relegate your mind to its proper place as *your tool,* you will ultimately see who you are.

Before gaining control over your mind, your relationship with it is like the person born and raised in a room with a television set playing loudly. He does not know he is able and supposed to turn the machine off when he doesn't feel like hearing the same old programs over again. He does not know how to turn the television off and rest himself from its tyranny.

The need for gaining control of the mind should be uppermost in your thoughts. The intellectual mind is the cause of every dissension.

Self-hypnosis quiets the mind, clearing it of wasteful content. It calms your nerves, and when practiced sincerely, along with your other physical and mental exercises, produces insight into the nature of yourself.

If we have aroused a bit of new determination in you, good! Now it is time for your next lesson in self-hypnosis. In this practice session, we will direct our attention towards the heavy drinker.

Have you thought about the time you took your first drink of alcohol? Did you find great relief from tension after that drink? Did you lose your fear of people? Were you suddenly able to mix easily with strangers? Do you understand why you drink when you don't want to drink? Is it in anticipation of the sense of relief you once experienced but no longer can count on after a drink? You now need more and more alcohol to reach that level of relaxation. Do you sometimes miss the mark and drink way beyond that point?

Are your fears a result of an early childhood experience? Are you harboring certain guilts? Do you suffer guilt and remorse over drinking?

The following is the self-hypnosis technique for the person who wants to control his drinking or give it up entirely. This time, we will use a *white dot* as the point of concentration.

Concentrate On White Dot

Just get comfortable. Let your body relax, let your mind relax, and shut your eyes.

"I want you to concentrate on making your mind go deeper and deeper, relax your body, go deeper and deeper asleep. I want you to imagine that your mind is floating down through the soft velvety blackness like a feather, floating down, way down, softly, gently, irresistibly, deeper, deeper, deeper, and deeper relaxed. Very, very comfortable, very, very relaxed, very, very pleasant. Actually feel the sensation of your mind going deeper and deeper, deeper, and deeper relaxed, all the way to the bottom, way down. Quietly, deeper, deeper, deeper, relaxed all

62

the way to the bottom. I'm going to count from ten down to one. As I count, make your mind, your body more deeply relaxed until by the time I reach the count of one take a very deep breath, blow all the way out, completely, deeply relaxed. Completely, deeply asleep.

"Ten . . . nine . . . eight . . . seven . . . six five . . . four . . . three . . . two . . . one . . . all the way down . . .way down.

"Now you know what I say is the absolute truth. When you sleep deeply enough, you can control your body, you can control your mind, you can do anything you make up your mind to do.

"Now I want you to concentrate on a white dot in the center of your forehead. A white dot in the center of your forehead; concentrate on it, see it, concentrate on it, see it. You actually see a white dot in the center of your forehead; you see nothing else but a white dot in the center of your forehead. Actually feel the sensation of your mind drifting out towards that white dot, drifting out closer and closer to that white dot, and now you go into a state of self-hypnosis and you know what I say is the actual truth.

Give Up Alcohol

"By giving up alcohol you are going to be rewarded by feeling better physically and mentally. You will admit to yourself now you do have a drinking problem and you will become determined to overcome it. You will no longer depend on someone else to make you stop drinking. You are going to stop of your own accord because you really, sincerely want to.

"You will remind yourself constantly of what you have learned and what you now understand through autoanalysis concerning your excessive drinking. From now on, you are going to find healthier outlets for your frustrations; you're going to do this on a day-to-day basis. From now on, you are going to practice the art of self-hypnosis so that you will never have to depend on alcohol again to relax you.

"You are never again going to fool yourself by thinking you can again handle that first drink of alcohol because you know now that you cannot. You will repeat to yourself, I must, I can, I will give up drinking entirely. You will say to yourself every day, in every way, I'm getting better and better.

"You will say to yourself, I now understand the primitive emotions for which I seek relief and outlet. But I will not give way to them—my conscious mind will not permit it. You will say to yourself, I know that knowledge is power—and I now have the knowledge that alcohol will only release my inhibitions and set my mind free for a temporary period. I now know that the anxieties will return after that drink wears off. I now know that I do not desire that false personality that alcohol will temporarily give me. I now know that what I want is a complete cure from the need for alcohol. I now know that alcohol is nothing more than a crutch—something that will help me for but a few moments.

"You now feel very relaxed, very confident, very sure of yourself. You are very proud of yourself that you now have in your possession this knowledge about your drinking habit.

"Anytime you wish to reproduce this feeling of relaxation, this feeling of confidence, this knowledge that alcohol is actually your enemy and not your friend—all you have to do and all you will do is grasp your left thumb with your right hand. Instantly upon contact of your right hand with your left thumb, your entire body will relax, your entire mind will relax, and instantly you will feel confident, calm, sure of yourself—you will feel exactly as though you have just had two stiff drinks of alcohol. The sensation will be the same, you will feel as though you have just had those two drinks—and therefore you will *know* that you do not need to have them.

"I want you to now grasp your left thumb with your right hand and actually experience the feeling of having just had two stiff drinks. You are very, very calm, very relaxed, very confident.

"And you know you can do anything you make up your mind to do without alcohol. You have no need for alcohol. You have no desire for alcohol. You know now that you yourself can accomplish the same feeling of tranquility, of confidence, of peace of mind —*without* the use of alcohol.

"I want you to awaken now free from pain or bodily discomfort, relaxed, calm, and confident in every way. You will waken on the count of three feeling as though you have just had a nice relaxing three hour nap. One—two —three. Awake!"

Review

Let us review what you have learned thus far.

1. You will accept voluntarily a suggestion while you are in a hypnotic state.

2. Your suggestibility will be heightened while you are in a hypnotic state.

3. You must be *willing* to be hypnotized and also willing to accept the suggestions you will be giving yourself.

4. You have now practiced with your powers of concentration. Have you completed the candle light exercise at least three times?

5. You have learned and memorized the procedure for self-relaxation. Did you actually feel your mind and your body relaxing? Practice it again; make sure you have all the key phrases committed to memory.

6. You have now learned that self-hypnosis is not a gift only certain people possess. It is a science recognized and practiced throughout the medical community.

7. You have had an opportunity to autoanalyze yourself and pinpoint your particular problem.

8. You have had an opportunity to communicate with your subconscious mind after you have completely relaxed yourself.

9. You have learned that such habits as excessive drinking and smoking can be conquered through the practice of self-hypnosis.

10. You have learned that most undesirable

habits such as drinking and smoking to excess are generally born in the subconscious—and you know now that what the mind causes the mind can cure.

If you are totally convinced you have now mastered the techniques so far described in this book—then it is time to proceed. Perhaps you should thumb through the previous pages and re-read the important highlights of the self-hypnosis experience.

Chapter 6

BREATHE DEEPLY AND FREELY AGAIN

We will now get into the subject of breathing. Yes, you read it correctly; the word is *breathing*. Before you attempt to induce a total state of hypnotic self-relaxation, it is of prime importance that you concentrate on your breathing. (This is especially necessary if your motivation for self-therapy is eliminating a smoking habit or a sexual problem).

We will call it the *whole breath* technique.

The principle behind the physical movements of the *whole breath* exercise can be stated in one sentence: You can only be certain of filling a sack completely by opening the sack before pouring in the contents.

Let us use a simple, practical example to illustrate what you will be thinking about while practicing this technique. You will imagine a grocery bag which you wish to fill with grain. The bottom half of this paper bag is crumpled. If you were to pour grain, no matter how finely ground, into this bag, only a few grains would trickle through to the bottom. The bulk of it would start filling the bag from the point just above the crumpled area.

In this same manner, if the bottom of the lungs are contracted, inhaled air will not reach the bottom. The lungs will commence to fill from a point midway or higher. It is impossible to get full use of the lungs.

The point is if you want to fill the lungs with air, you must first expand them so the air being inhaled will go directly to the bottom of the lungs, filling up the deepest recesses.

Whole Breath Exercise

Set the chair in a room in a section of your home where you can be reasonably certain you will not be disturbed by other members of the family, the telephone, or street noises.

Lower the lights. If you prefer, turn on some relaxing music.

Take three deep breaths. Breath deeply and slowly.

All breathing is to be done through the nostrils.

It is necessary to master three bodily movements in order to be able to perform the *whole breath* technique.

1. Exhale slightly through your nostrils. Commence inhaling through your nose while making the following movement: push down and out with your diaphragm.

The diaphragm is the sheet of muscle that separates your chest cavity from your abdomen. The process of pushing this diaphragm down and out consists of "making a big belly." Push your abdominal region out as far as you can. This automatically draws the diaphragm outward. Remember to push your abdomen downward at the same time.

2. To begin your formal practice of the whole breath technique, allow five seconds for this first movement.

Still inhaling slowly, smoothly, and quietly, in the next five seconds perform the following movement:

Bring your extended abdomen *in* until it feels taut, and at the same time spread your ribs, expanding your entire rib cage.

To expand your rib cage correctly, push forward with your breastbone and attempt to spread your ribs outward at the sides. As with most of these techniques, you will get the feel of it quickly and you will know when you are performing it correctly.

3. The third bodily movement of the whole breath exercise is as follows:

Still inhaling slowly and quietly, place your finger tips on your chest, resting them lightly, so that you can still feel the expansion of your chest as you breathe.

As you inhale, the abdomen is pulled tightly

in at this point and held tightly in until the next breath begins, when the diaphragm must once again be extended down and out.

This third movement, ending with the complete raising of the shoulders, will also be performed to the count of five seconds.

4. So far, one slow, quiet inhalation of breath has been taken for the count of fifteen seconds. During this fifteen-second inhalation, the three movements just described have been performed, each movement taking five seconds. Both the movements and the inhalations are to be executed in a smooth, continuous manner.

5. At this point you will hold your breath in for the count of ten seconds, concentrating on your buttocks. This manipulation consists of closing the anal sphincters tightly by squeezing the buttocks and drawing the anal sphincters upward.

The breath is now expelled in a controlled manner, slowly, smoothly, and quietly, the shoulders being lowered in the same way in which they were raised. The exhalation should be performed in this quiet, controlled manner to the count of fifteen seconds.

To sum up the whole breath relaxation technique:

Inhale to the count of fifteen, performing the three movements as described.

Retain your breath for the count of ten.

Exhale to the count of fifteen with no special movements, simply relaxing the posture that was assumed. Do not, however, collapse or allow your breath to gush out. Exhale slowly and easily. This is essential to the success of relaxation through breathing. When you have finished exhaling and are ready to inhale the next whole breath, you should be in the same sitting position as when you began. Your body will quickly adapt itself to this technique and the movements which you are teaching it.

Do the whole breath exercise three to five times before your regular self-hypnosis session and before you practice any of the techniques taught in this book.

If done correctly, you should experience a relaxation immediately enjoyable and restful.

The whole breath exercise may be performed as many times as you are able to do it during the day. The exaggerated movement of raising your shoulders is not necessary if you are away from the privacy of your home. You may practice while sitting, standing, walking, or even driving your car.

We have all seen the athlete who is going to take what he believes to be a complete or deep breath.

He takes a mighty inhalation, making a tremendous chest and at the same time pulling his abdomen up and in. You can now see the fallacy of such a method. Pulling the abdomen in compresses the lower part of the lungs. Only by the whole breath movements can the lungs be opened in a correct fashion to enable air to fill them completely.

Extending the abdomen, which pushes the diaphragm down and out, frees the lower portion of the lungs. Spreading the ribs, in the second part of the inhalation movement, allows the middle portion of the lungs to be filled completely too. Raising the shoulders in the third part of the

72

inhalation exercise enables the air to fill the upper portions of the lungs and reach those seldom aerated lobes so susceptible to tuberculosis.

In the performance of this technique you have been *concentrating* and breathing correctly while relaxing. The average person breathes far too quickly—from fifteen to twenty-two times a minute—and far too shallowly—the air trickling in no further than the top third of the lung. Oxygen is a primary source of nourishment and energy in your blood stream. The slower and more completely you breath, the longer you will live, and the healthier you will be. You will feel calm and more alert. The mere act of *concentrating* on your breathing will prepare you for the self-induced hypnotic session you will enter into.

Those who smoke will find this technique especially useful. In fact, if you practice the whole breath technique for a sufficient length of time, you will find that one day upon picking up a cigarette you will be unable to smoke it. The lungs will have been cleansed of coal tar residue and other impurities to such an extent your organism will be revolted by the cigarette fumes.

Those who do not have the smoking habit are still subjected to gasoline and noxious chemical fumes. This daily exercise helps counteract the toxic, draining effects of these impurities.

Now we suggest that you re-read the whole breath technique and practice it one or two times. It will be step one in the self-hypnosis session you have already committed yourself to on a daily basis.

If you have ever taken singing lessons, you may already be familiar with this technique. If you have not, and since long, slow breaths will be a part of your daily autorelaxation sessions, it is best to learn the proper method from the outset.

Now let me try and guess what you are saying:

"Wait a minute! At the beginning, you told me that this self-hypnosis session would only require five minutes of my time per day. You are now instructing me to do a breathing exercise first, concentrate on a candle with my eyes open for three minutes and then closed for three minutes, and try the autorelaxation technique involving all sorts of suggestions to relax myself. I am to concentrate on a white dot in the center of my forehead, and we haven't even reached the stage of posthypnotic suggestion. This sounds to me like it's going to take about an hour of my time each day."

Not so. The breathing exercise comes to a total of one-hundred and twenty seconds or two minutes.

The three-minute eyes-opened-eyes-closed candle concentration was only a rehearsal to teach you to concentrate on one object. If you have indeed practiced it five separate times, you can now limit your candle gazing to twenty seconds with your eyes open and twenty seconds with your eyes closed. The subconscious mind now has the message—it will perform the ritual almost by itself.

The autorelaxation procedure, if you have committed it totally to memory, will take less than a minute and a half. Your subconscious mind has by this time become *accustomed* to the repeated suggestions of relaxation, and both your mind and body will relax instantaneously, perhaps before the suggestion is dictated to it.

The concentration on the white dot in the center of your forehead should now take, after rehearsal, no more than ten seconds.

That leaves you thirty full seconds to give yourself the auto-therapy instructions and suggestions.

For instance, time yourself. If your problem is the smoking habit for example—how long does it take you to say to yourself:

"You will reject from your mind any desire to smoke a cigarette. From this moment on, the taste of a cigarette will be disgusting to you. For the next 48 hours you will feel completely relaxed, extremely calm, and totally confident, knowing you can do anything you make up your mind to do. And you will not smoke a cigarette, nor desire one."

The whole process took exactly five minutes, correct?

After you have practiced the method of relaxing yourself each day for thirty days, and you are convinced that complete relaxation can be accomplished through self-hypnosis, you will be able to use an extremely rapid method of autorelaxation. This involves the use of a key word or phrase such as "Relax." Or "Mind asleep—body asleep!" Or "I am a set of clothing hanging limply over a chair—completely limp—completely relaxed." Or simply, "Let go! Every muscle is letting go! Every nerve asleep!"

You will find that these suggestions, or better still, the suggestion *you* think up, will immediately set into motion the process of relaxation. Your subconscious mind will associate the words you choose as a signal suggesting all your muscles, from your head to your feet, are instantly becoming limp and relaxed.

Remember, the subconscious mind cannot reason. It will take simple direction at face value and react immediately, once trained.

The Rope Trick

It is time for a little experiment.

Seat yourself in a quiet and semi-dark room. Turn on some pleasant music.

Light the candle, sit back, and stare into it for twenty seconds.

Close your eyes and picture the candle in your mind's eye for another ten seconds.

Take the three deep and full breaths described in the whole breathing technique.

Give yourself the entire autorelaxation suggestion dialogue.

Picture the white dot in the center of your forehead and your mind drifting out towards that white dot.

Now say to yourself,

"You are going into a complete state of self-hypnosis, and you know what I say is the absolute truth. You are feeling a rope being tied *tightly* around your right wrist. It is tied so tight it burns slightly. And now that rope is lifting your wrist and your arm towards the ceiling. You try not to let your arm be lifted, but the rope is pulling upward very hard, upward . . . pulling upward . . . pulling upward . . . the rope is pulling your wrist and your arm slowly upward and you cannot resist as your arm goes upward . . .

pulling upward . . . pulling upward . . .

"You try not to let your arm go upward but you cannot stop it as the rope pulls upward . . . upward! Higher! Your arm going higher! The rope is pulling your wrist higher!

"All right the rope is released and you can put your arm down now. I want you to awaken on the count of three feeling normal and relaxed in every way, your body free from pain or discomfort and knowing that you can do anything that you make up your mind to do. One—two getting brighter your mind is getting brighter—three and you're awake!"

You have, once again, experienced a light stage of self-hypnosis. Your own personal degree of suggestibility can be measured by how high your wrist and arm are elevated in the air at this point. You have also proven to yourself you can indeed hypnotize yourself. Were you really able to hold your arm down once that rope around your wrist got to hugging at it?

If you need further proof of your own vulnerability to suggestion, there are other tests you might want to give yourself. For instance, after going through the process of candle staring, the whole breath technique, the autorelaxation procedure, etc., try telling yourself in a firm voice, "You will simply have to swallow the saliva in your mouth in the next ten seconds. You must swallow now. You will swallow now!"

Were you able to resist the impulse to swallow?

But let us not forget something! Be certain you say to yourself, after every experiment of actual autohypnosis session:

77

"You will awaken now on the count of three feeling normal, relaxed, free from pain or body discomfort in every way. One—two—getting brighter—three and awake!"

Chapter 7

THE POWER OF
POSITIVE SUGGESTIONS

We are getting the unconscious mind in our
sights, and we're almost ready to fire on it. We
have learned the unconscious mind by itself, or
under external influence, can direct behavior. It
is possible to use this to your own advantage. In
the case of hysteria, we see the unconscious mind
negatively autosuggesting. For example, the ap-
prehensive student suggests to himself that he or
she knows absolutely nothing as a school examination approaches. This is the kind of hysteria we
intend to combat.

Our weapon is beneficial autosuggestion. Confidence, optimism, and expectation of cure are the bullets we will be firing into our subconscious mind from now on.

Autosuggestion is not a direct expression of willpower; it is an exercise of imagination and faith. People have to be distracted if they want to free themselves from obsessions. To believe one has *arrived* is the success of autosuggestion. Autosuggestion is a psychological art. It is this art we are teaching you, step by step.

We could have given you the simple procedure for self-hypnosis in the first ten pages if autosuggestion were merely a direct expression of willpower. It would have been quite easy to tell you, "Determine to defeat your troubles." However, it's not that simple.

Suggestion consists of reflex conditioning. A person learns to activate his brain, so the conscious mind is incapable of opposing it.

We do not teach a child by saying to him, "You will learn math, you will, you will!" Instead we teach the child by repeating, "One and one are two, two and two are four, three and three are six . . ." Isn't it true reflex conditioning caused you to continue and say to yourself, "and four and four are eight"? You have been *conditioned* by reflex action. Now we must condition your reflex action to think healthy, think confidently, think happy, think optimistically. It will require continual stimulation and exercise.

Self-hypnosis is a *strong* stimulation.

Self-hypnosis is a *beneficial* exercise.

Now read those last two lines over again.

Read them once more.

After you have read them half a dozen times, you will have a stronger belief in these two statements than you did the first time you read them.

Because of the repetition, your conscious mind has become unable to oppose the suggestion. It is fortunate the two statements are true, and by believing them, you will be strengthened in your purpose of attaining self-help through self-hypnosis.

The unconscious itself is very fragile. We will attempt here to prove it.

You will recall the long lines of people waiting for hours outside motion picture theaters where *The Exorcist* was shown. Once inside the theater, some patrons didn't remain seated long. The story of a 12-year-old girl possessed by the devil, and the efforts to exorcise the devil turned the strongest stomachs. The manager of one theater commented, "It's amazing to me that grown people, successful in their fields, can react this way. It's like this every night. The men faint, and the women vomit."

Suggestion is at work again. There is a good deal of vomiting and fainting in the film.

Effects of Repetition

While on the subject of this controversial motion picture, I cannot resist telling the story a close friend of mine related recently.

I know his wife is prudish and a deeply religious woman. I have never heard her utter even the word "damn" in conversation. How my friend ever lured his wife to see *The Exorcist,* I'll never know. They went into a cocktail lounge and over their drinks (she had a Shirley Temple; she never touches alcohol), he asked her, "You know, I missed the scene where the kid attacked the doctor. What is it she did to him?"

Without blinking an eye, his wife replied, "She grabbed him by the . . ." and she named a slang word used for the penis. My friend was never so shocked in his life. In their twelve years of married life, he had never heard his wife use that kind of language. She immediately opened her eyes wide, blushed, and apologized, "I don't know what made me say that!"

But we know: suggestion.

The woman had just been in a crowded theater for two hours, during which period the word used had become acceptable dialogue, repeated innumerable times. Her unconscious mind became used to the idea that such a word was not offensive or embarrassing at all, although all of her previous life she had shunned the use of such language.

This experience can be translated. How many times in your life have you had to say, "I don't know what in the world made me do or say that." It is possible that some exiled suggestion fleetingly visited your conscious mind and directed it?

Insomnia

Frank S. Caprio, M.D., in his research on insomnia, lists seven main causes of sleepless nights:

Worry, labeling oneself an insomniac, nervous fatigue, pain and discomfort from illness, poor sleeping conditions (soft mattress, noise, etc.), guilt feelings, and disorganized thinking. To combat all these problems over one billion sleeping pills are sold yearly.

A great many people suffer from insomnia. In some cases, the insomniac's thinking gets caught up in a circular treadmill. He can't get off it. He keeps reworking the same thought, problem, or fear over and over again.

In the case of Patricia, she was twenty-seven years old and unmarried. She still lived with her parents. Actually she had two problems on her mind. Would she ever find a mate and what could she possibly do about her inability to get to sleep for hours after she retired for the night?

The two problems, as it turned out, were unrelated. She was an attractive woman, but just had not met "Mr. Right" yet. Living in the suburbs of Los Angeles, she had been somewhat limited in meeting new people. She decided, and her mother agreed, that she should move into her own apartment in Hollywood, where she would meet more men.

She went apartment hunting. As she looked at one apartment after another, she realized that it was important to her to live at least one story off the street. She found just such an apartment, and what was even more significant, the downstairs main entrance was locked after ten at night.

That would certainly take care of the reoccurring nightmare that a man was slipping into her bedroom. In this nightmare she was never able to scream, never even able to raise herself from her bed to beg this intruder not to hurt her. She had lived with the nightmare for a long time. It wasn't all that important. It was a part of sleep, and she became used to it. But not being able to fall asleep was something to which she could not accustom herself. It affected her work, her dating, even her attitude toward her co-workers.

Once in her own apartment, Pat became depressed, lost weight, and became obsessed with fear that every night for the rest of her life would be like this—trying so hard to go to sleep, but not being able to.

Pat was afraid of sleep, afraid of that nightmare.

After a year of this torture, she found herself sitting at bars until they closed, rather than go home and face sleep.

Pat worked at the reception desk of a Hollywood beauty parlor, a new job she had acquired after moving out of her parents' home. Fortunate for Pat, one of the steady customers was a nurse who worked in the nearby office of a medical doctor who practiced hypnosis.

Pat, under that doctor's guidance, learned she could attain the hypnotic state of relaxation and that she could go to sleep in mid-afternoon in the doctor's office. Under the doctor's care she learned the technique of self-hypnosis, and was able to employ the relaxation suggestions in her own bed at night. In Pat's case, her doctor recorded a tape for her with soft piano music in the background. Pat soon found she could not think about the hypnotic suggestions on the relaxing tape and also think about the intruder nightmare that was sure to come, once she got to sleep.

After a week of listening to the self-hypnosis

tape, Pat found sleep just naturally came over her. After two weeks, she began to say the words to herself, as soon as she got into bed. She didn't need the tape anymore. Her subconscious mind expected sleep when she got into bed.

We wish we could tell you that Pat found her "Mr. Right," and is now happily married. She may well be, but we do not know that part of the story. But we do know that self-hypnosis solved Pat's insomnia problem.

The mind cannot concentrate on more than one thing at a time. It is not built to do so. If you want to prove it, try memorizing the lyrics to a song you are listening to on the radio, and read a paragraph of a book at the same time.

If you're concentrating on a specific problem, a particularly aggravating person, or a lover, you cannot possibly concentrate on what you got into bed for in the first place: sleep. You didn't lock your troubles in your dresser drawer before you got into bed. After all, you can't do anything about those troubles in bed while the night slips by. Unless you are troubled by an actual pain or discomfort from illness, you should *expect* to go to sleep immediately.

Perhaps you have labeled yourself an insomniac, and that's just the type of negative suggestion we've been talking about. Like Patricia, you're reinforcing that negative suggestion each night by obsessively thinking you just can't sleep.

If you're worrying during the night about what you did or said during the day or last week or last year, then you really need to reinforce the suggestion that the past is the past, and the past is gone, dead, over with. There is nothing you can do about what you said or what you did. The problem will find its own answer tomorrow. Scarlet O'Hara in *Gone With The Wind* said, "I'll think about that tomorrow." Clever, that Scarlet. She wasn't foolish enough to lose the sleep her body and mind needed.

Sleeping Made Easy

Look at your bed before you get into it. You bought it or rented it for the purpose of sleep, not for the purpose of worrying. Okay, so now we know what the bed is for.

Get into bed and assume your most familiar and comfortable position.

Concentrate on only one thing, and that one thing is:

The relaxation suggestions of your self-hypnosis procedure, with emphasis on the sinking down into the *soft, velvety darkness,* and the mind *drifting out toward that white dot.*

"Want sleep. Be willing to accept sleep. Tell yourself you are willing to accept sleep.

"Tell yourself that sleep is so beautiful, so deep, so refreshing, and it is very much like the aftermath of satisfying sexual intercourse.

"And now suggest to yourself that, you like yourself, and therefore you want to give yourself the wonderful gift of sleep, *deep refreshing sleep.* Think about the *soft velvety darkness again.* See it. Picture it. See your mind drifting down into it. Don't concentrate too hard. Just let it happen. So nice. So peaceful. So velvety in its darkness, its tranquility.

Buddah said, "Release is in the eyes." Your eyes can actually be staring and tense, even though your eyelids are closed. When you want to sleep, practice relaxing your eyes.

"Close your eyes and take a deep breath . . . in . . . in. Hold it for a moment. Exhale and relax all the muscles about your eyes. Relax all the muscles above your eyes. Now feel all the muscles below the eyes relaxing. Feel all the muscles at the corner of your eyes, and in between your eyes, relaxing . . . relaxing . . . relaxing . . . relaxing. Your eyelids are so relaxed that they just won't work. They are closed. Deeply closed and contentedly closed. Use the tremendous power of your imagination and pretend that no matter how hard you try, your eyelids WANT to remain closed, you cannot open them.

The tongue is one of the strongest muscles in the body. It is also one of the most tense. Think about your own tongue at this very moment. Relax it . . . relax it . . . relax it.

"Keep your tongue away from the roof of your mouth or your teeth. Picture your tongue away from the roof of your mouth or your teeth. Picture your tongue as a limp muscle that is melting . . . melting . . . melting.

"Pretend your whole heart and soul are *so relaxed* you just cannot open them. Stop trying to open them now . . . and slip deeper into the soft velvety darkness of wonderful, refreshing sleep . . . going deeper . . . deeper. Use the tremendous powers of your imagination to *pretend* that no matter how hard the outside tries, you just cannot resist the beauty of the sleep that is just seconds away from you. Now *promise* yourself a beautiful dream while floating down through the soft, velvety darkness of sweet, delightful sleep.

"And sink deeper . . . *deeper* . . . deeper, into the sweet, soft . . . velvety darkness. Eyes completely relaxed . . . tongue loose and relaxed . . . not touching anything . . . and as the tongue relaxes, hangs loose, so does the entire body . . . and you calmly . . . quietly . . . call upon sleep to come . . .

"To come . . . and slip peacefully into your wonderful world . . ."

Insomnia is one of the easiest problems to treat through hypnosis, because the hypnotic state and sleep are so much alike.

Now read over the insomnia exercise and practice it. It may take diligent practice, but eventually you will be able to do it. Sleep will come. Even if your problem is not insomnia, you may experience a restful nap at this point.

After some successful practice with this exercise, you will also be able to add another step—autosuggestion of post-hypnosis. You will be able to tell yourself *how long* you will sleep, at what time you will awaken, and that when you awaken you will feel refreshed, alert, and alive with new energy!

Chapter 8

YOU AND YOUR SEX PROBLEM

It is unfortunate this chapter must carry such a heading, but in America the very word *sex* is a problem. During childhood and adolescence we are actually taught sex is a problem. Very little is said about sex being good, or being fun, a repeatable human *joy*. Americans make jokes about it being hot and spicy, in an indirect and backhanded sort of way. Above the table come the warnings, the cautions, "What about your reputation, abortion, illegitimate pregnancy, syphillis, gonorrhea, perversions, and mental breakdown?" Is it any wonder that the psychotherapist's office is forever besieged by disturbed people, most of whom suffer from some degree of sexual anxiety?

Say the word sex and it's like pushing a button that lights up distress signals on the mind's switchboard. *Fear. Guilt.*

Society can look the other way, nose upturned, if it likes, but the fact is we pet, indulge in masturbation, fornication, adultery, and homosexual acts almost universally.

All too often, we engage in sex in hiding—stealthily, guiltily. We've been *trained* that way, which results in frigidity, impotence, guilt, and fear. These problems are passed from the adolescent boy and girl to the adult man and woman. Is sex good or bad—is it delicious or distasteful? These words create conflict. Conflict means indecision which in turn causes fear.

It's a case of damned if you do and damned if you don't.

Boys and girls are taught they must win in the social game of getting along with the opposite sex. How are they supposed to learn that lesson without experience? Teen-agers are as afraid of the sex act as they are of their report card grade in algebra, yet they have been *taught* the algebra lesson, but no one has given them a lesson in sex. This leads to fear, ineptness, and inhibition. These are the ingredients young adults carry right into marriage. And then it is a very real problem. Anxiety, despair, and neurosis are at the root of many broken marriages.

You can end this vicious cycle in your own life, through self-hypnosis.

Assuming you have a sexual hang-up, concentrate on the problem *after* you have gone through the steps to induce the state of hypnotic self-relaxation. Think about it. During the self-analysis stage, try and understand what your particular sexual maladjustment is all about, where it comes from, how it started, and how it has developed. Does it stem from a neurotic parental influence? A past sexual transgression you are ashamed of and feel guilty about? What was it? Were you ever caught masturbating? Or did you torment yourself with the fear of being caught? Did you have a wet dream, and you had to stealthily hide the soiled sheet? Infidelity? You enjoyed it at the time but later felt it was perverse or lustful?

Ask yourself if any of this is standing in the way of you and the natural enjoyment you should be experiencing in your sex relations with your partner. Ask yourself if you are the victim of a certain attitude toward sex or an isolated experience in your life.

Accept the posthypnotic suggestion that the door is now closed on the past. Forgive yourself. Say it over and over,

"You are forgiven, and you will reject the past fears and guilts from your mind. You can and will enjoy sex. Exaggerated feelings of guilt, false modesty, shyness, and the like are stupid, and you know you are not a stupid person."

In this simple sex problem hypnosis lesson we have dealt with the spectrum of sex in a general way. *Attitude* seems to be the key word here. What is your attitude regarding sex?

Has your unconscious convinced you that you

do not have the ability to love or that you are not a good lover?

Love is an emotion that begins within yourself; it starts with self-love. Love for a member of the opposite sex commences with the love of yourself. Turn that inferiority complex regarding how good a lover you are around. Under hypnosis, convince yourself you are an accomplished sexual partner. Repeat the suggestion, until it becomes an ingrained attitude. Once convinced, you will love yourself a little more than you did before. You will automatically be more capable of loving someone else.

Have you built up defense barriers—walls of prudishness around your sex life? You have a mistaken attitude. This can easily lead to frigidity. We *can* correct our thinking. Frigidity *can* be cured. Sex is beautiful, not nasty. Sex is natural, not painful. Sex is a reward, not a submission.

In the writing of this chapter, interviews were held with a marriage counselor and a psychotherapist, specializing in sex-related problems. The following represents some of their remarks in response to a set of prepared questions.

Sex: A Man's View

"I would guess I've interviewed several thousand husbands about their sex frustrations and inner yearnings. It is always more difficult to get a man to talk about sex than it is to lead a woman into the subject, by that I mean a discussion of their personal attitudes, not sex in general. Men have a tendency to want to approach the subject of sex from a comedy standpoint—

jokes and stories. This is a defense mechanism, a substitute for revealing their own sexual experiences, thoughts, and inhibitions. Women, on the other hand, seem to want to talk about themselves and the particular perplexity or disappointment troubling them personally.

"On the other hand, we know males are much more involved with sexual thoughts than women —their drives and desires are stronger, and they are more rapidly aroused sexually than women. These emotions in men are instantly explosive— can be set off by the stimulation of a beautiful pair of legs, a half-exposed bosom, an erotic book. This very often produces fear in men: fear they will lose control, and reveal their true selves. So they build up defense mechanisms, on-guard attitudes, if you like, which keep the subject of sex on an impersonal level.

"If you walk into an erotic book store, you will always find men looking through the racks, not women. The erotic fiction and provocative jackets don't involve the men personally.

"In bed, however, the man is himself involved, and he is still very often on guard to prevent an eruption of his emotions. In a certain sense, love and tenderness are completely separated from sex in a man's mind. Not so with a woman. To her, they are one and the same thing. Put all these forces to work in the same bed, and is it any wonder you have a skyrocketing divorce rate?

"What usually happens is the wife gets the impression from her husband that the sexual experience is strictly impersonal, and she is being used. The humiliation often builds in her unconscious mind, and she climbs into bed thinking of herself as a thing instead of a partner in a wonderful experience. What has happened is her desire to surrender fades. On the other hand, the desire to conquer, intrinsic in the male, has also been suppressed by his fear of revealing his true self. They are no longer playing their traditional roles.

"I saw your raised eyebrows when I said that word tradition, but isn't it true that a man often offers love in order to get sex, and a woman often offers sex in order to get love? You know, a man has an extra burden put on him in the sex act. He has to prove his masculinity to himself. In the heat of the sex act, his pride is more involved than anything else, probably one of the reasons why men are more sensitive about their performance.

"As a marriage counselor, I can tell you the problem of impotence is far more shattering to the male ego than frigidity is to the female's.

"If a woman really loves a man, she will try to understand this sensitivity. It is sometimes hard for a woman to comprehend. She has no experience within her own makeup to compare to it. If she is foolish enough to react with contempt, then the odds are increased tenfold they will end up in divorce court—for that is the ultimate of shattering experiences for the husband. A husband expects his wife to want to be conquered. If he offers to conquer her, and she refuses, there is no other road for the husband's pride to travel but that of humiliation. You have a badly wounded ego on your hands.

"Now let me tell you about another balancing factor that is built into the male personality.

It is the male's sensitivity regarding being capable of bringing his sex partner to a successful orgasm. If she doesn't go over the edge, he feels he has failed in another way.

"Just as wives often don't understand the husband's ego, the husband doesn't understand the orgasm is not as important to the woman as it is to the man. The male feels his prestige has been damaged. He may not brave sex again for a couple of weeks or a month. Then you've got a suspicious wife on your hands, a wife convinced hubby doesn't love her, doesn't desire her any more. So, it takes an adjustment on both parts. The burden is the husband's for it takes self-control on the part of the husband. And in sex, self-control for the male doesn't come naturally. Women should express their appreciation for their mate's effort and self-control in building up to a mutual sexual climax. This rebuilds his ego and makes him feel he is a good bed partner. If he is feeling good, she will be feeling good. If he is feeling proud, she is feeling satisfied. Sex isn't everything in marriage, but other problems disappear once partners come to a meeting of the minds, as well as a meeting of the bodies."

Are you a man who is oversensitive about sex? Have you tried to keep the subject at arm's length because of some inferiority complex you've nursed for years?

Or are you a female, who, until now, has been unable to understand the driving forces your mate is wrestling with?

Decide what posthypnotic suggestion you're going to give yourself. Self-hypnosis *can* correct your thinking.

Eighty-five percent of all frigidity problems are caused by psychological factors. You can control your mind, you can control your body . . . through self-hypnosis.

Tension during the sex act is a product of the unconscious mind. The odds are high tension is an outgrowth of misinformation, earlier in life.

The door on the past is closed. You have a whole new and wonderful experience approaching the next time you and your mate commit yourself to the rewards of a totally satisfying sex act. Tell yourself you will now look forward to that new experience. It is nature's intention you enjoy sex. It is nature's intention you love yourself and therefore can love someone else. Your sexual responses will improve. You will express your appreciation for your mate's lovemaking ability. As a husband, you will be able to control yourself (but with the prolonged enjoyment that will bring) until your wife is moved to the same state of arousal you are experiencing.

It has been said the mind influences the heart beat, as the heart pumps blood through the veins.

Picture, under sef-hypnosis, blood flowing through your veins. Direct the flow of blood to the genital organs. Feel the energy in your body being directed toward that point, feel the warmth of the blood and the energy in that area. The feedback from these suggestions will be an erotic input into your unconscious and will intensify your sexual responses.

There is nothing shameful about sex.

Sex: A Woman's View

Of course, whenever you get into the subject of

sex, you are bound to run into many opinions. After the interview with the marriage counselor quoted, it occurred to me that the entire presentation leaned toward telling only the man's view of sex. For that reason, I looked forward to my next interview with a woman psychotherapist noted for her investigations into sex behavior and sex-related problems. I present her comments here not to confuse you, but to afford you the opportunity to determine what line of thinking is best suited to your particular problem.

"The timing of a book on self-hypnosis is perfect. You know, meditation is big on the campuses now. Self-hypnosis is closely related to meditation, and it can be a soothing experience. In answer to your question on the subject of frigidity, you're not going to like what I have to say, I'm afraid. A high degree of female frigidity problems presented in my office are usually caused by male attitudes and practices.

"Many of the so-called frigidity cases are not frigidity problems at all. It usually begins with a visit by the woman who claims she is sexually frozen. Question her carefully, and you find out that she, the woman, is as capable of orgasm as her husband is, in many cases, even more capable. The trouble is she has come to *think* of herself in a distorted and warped way, actually imagining she is incompetent sexually.

"Where did this notion come from in the first place? From her husband, of course. It seems the male animal has constructed a theory of female orgasm that does little more than give his own ego a lift. He has talked himself into the mistaken opinion his wife *should* be as easily satisfied in coitus as he is. Let the wife *not* reach satisfaction, and the husband then and there decides she must be neurotic or at least immature. Trouble is they don't have a name for this neurosis—or pseudo-neurosis would be more correct—and so they grab onto the word *frigid*.

"It is simply a case of the man not knowing penile stimulation of the vaginal muscles will not always cause a complete or full orgasm in the female. It is all very neat and in place that stimulation of the male organ will almost always result in orgasm.

"Many women, in the course of their entire lives, rarely or never experience that kind of climax. But the truth of the matter is that most of these same women are experiencing perfectly fine orgasms all of their lives. The man quotes from oddball books he's read, and soon it's no longer speculation—even in the wife's mind. She honestly believes there must be something wrong with her. She has been convinced she is *supposed* to have a climax just the same, and just as often as her husband. Know what those thoughts lead to? She puts a mental throttle on the whole thing and develops a block that actually *prevents* her from experiencing the sensation at all.

"It's the male attitude that has caused this. Because they are easily satisfied in coitus, they think their wives should be too. I find that most males who have this mistaken notion are poor lovers to begin with. A variation in technique seems unnecessary to them. They forget the need for preliminary lovemaking. Some of them are actually shocked to find out what techniques

98

their wives *really* desire. Then they call her sick in another way. The man has a picture of what the sex act should be in his own brain. These men also have fixed notions dinner should be ready when they arrive home; their shirts should be laundered and waiting. That's all a part of being sexually selfish too.

"Most of my so-called frigid women patients turn out to have large sexual capacities. The woman worries she won't have an obvious climax, and she knows this would displease her husband. The result is she has no climax at all. The mind tends to concentrate well on only one thing at a time. If a woman is worrying that *he* will be displeased, it diverts her thoughts from enjoying what is happening. The result is no orgasm, and hubby goes back to harping on the idea that something must be wrong with her. She better see a doctor. Actually it is his ego—or *lack* of it —that should be treated. He should *want* his wife to be satisfied, but he shouldn't *require* it, the way he does his dinner and his laundered shirts.

"The next step is the wife ends up in my clinic. Much to the wife's surprise, I usually have to insist upon talking to the husband. I'm not too popular with husbands, I'm afraid. Maybe because I make them face the real problem."

You have the points of view of two professionals—a man and a woman. Perhaps somewhere in their dialogue on sexual problems you can identify your set of circumstances and select the self-hypnotic suggestion that will afford you sexual harmony with your mate.

Now do the following:

1. Ask yourself what is at the core of your sex

problem. Be sure you are perfectly honest with yourself.

2. The breathing exercise.

3. The candle-glow exercise.

4. The auto-relaxation procedure.

5. The white-dot-in-the-center-of-the-forehead concentration.

6. The posthypnotic suggestions.

In most cases, you will be seeking to change your attitude toward sex, to develop confidence in yourself, to understand sex is to be enjoyed, and to close the door on past guilts. You will reject morbid sexual thoughts from your mind. It will become impossible for you to *remember* them. Past inner conflicts about sex have disappeared —flown away, never to return. In the midst of the sex act, wonderful relaxation and joy will come and enable you to achieve sexual satisfaction. You love yourself and so you are able to love another. You are sure of yourself and your love-making ability. You will compliment your mate on his/her lovemaking.

Autoanalysis has revealed the emotional factors responsible for the development of your particular sexual problem; therefore, you can now deal with the situation intelligently.

You can control your mind and your body!

You can do anything you make up your mind to do!

A Minister Speaks

An entirely different light was shed on the subject of sex problems as a result of an interview with a member of the clergy, also involved in marriage counseling.

"Let me say this; sex isn't everything. The sex balloon has been blown up to a point where sexual intercourse is promoted as a means for solving nonsexual problems. Sex is not the driving force of human beings, as a good many myths would have you believe. We get notions about ourselves that are in no way related to reality. As a result, some people seek sex as a cure for loneliness. The only cure for loneliness is the warmth and acceptance that comes from a much more meaningful relationship.

"Society has come to use sex for a reassurance of femininity or masculinity. The real values of life itself have little to do with sex. Sex is but an expression between people who love each other. There are so many other ways we can develop as human beings. Sexuality is only a small part of the total personality. You probably won't print this, it isn't a very popular approach."

Well, I did include it. I still happen to believe that love, although pretty old-fashioned an idea by modern standards, is a straight road towards the realization of true happiness.

Chapter 9

CONTROL YOUR SMOKING HABIT

Perhaps you should read no further if you are a heavy smoker and don't really want to give it up. This chapter might scare you.

Let us begin with a look at what nicotine really is and what it does.

Nicotine is a dangerous substance, no question about that. At the 34-nation First World Conference on Smoking and Health (1967), it was established that the activity of nicotine "would link smoking dependence with other major forms of dependence, such as heroin and alcohol."

Nicotine is a poisonous alkaloid, known in

chemistry as C10H14N2, a nerve drug which is so potent that a one-drop injection causes instant death. It does cause more deaths each year than the most infamous of hard drugs, heroin.

Inhale a cigarette, and you may very well be opening the door to an onslaught of cancer-producing agents, lung pollutants, and poisons. Three-hundred and sixty thousand known deaths are attributed to cigarette smoking yearly; 565 billion cigarettes are smoked each year. Each and every one of them is capable of contributing to death by emphysema; death by oxygen-starvation (broncho pulmonary diseases) ; death by heart stimulation (nicotine increases the heart beat 20 beats a minute in many cases) ; death by circulatory complication (vaso-constriction—one cigarette has been known to lower the temperature of the body's extremities as much as 10 degrees F.) ; and death from angina pectoris (a condition caused by a shock to the nerves of the heart).

At least seven known deadly emissions come from cigarette tobacco. That figure doesn't include at least fifteen volatile substances classified as either poisons or irritants. At the top of this killer list is hydrogen cyanide. Further down on the list, but just as dangerous, is carbon monoxide, present in amounts of at least one thousand times what is judged to be safe by environmental levels.

In two months more people die from cigarette smoking than died in twelve years of the Vietnam war, according to American casualty figures.

According to a British study, cigarette smoking now causes as many deaths as tuberculosis, typhoid, and cholera ever did.

All the epidemics of yellow fever ever recorded in medical history didn't cause as many deaths as cigarettes have in the United States alone in one single year!

The Addiction

But it is the addiction factor that we are combating here.

We will begin by getting a new picture of a cigarette deeply "burned" into your unconscious mind.

There is nothing glamorous about a cigarette, nothing glamorous about the smoking of one. This misconception was introduced in the now corny movies of the thirties and forties. If you wish evidence that smoking a cigarette in no way enhances your glamour, just take a look at the fingers you hold that poison with. Take a look at your teeth. Those nicotine stains are far from glamorous. Your breath is probably far from kissable. That chronic cough is far from appealing. By present day fashions, you no longer look worldly when you stick a cigarette between your lips. You look foolish, uninformed, and ignorant. You are annoying to others who have had the wisdom and courage to eliminate cigarettes from their world.

Reread the above paragraph. You will be using parts of it in your next hypnosis session. No one wants to be offensive to those around them, so the word *"annoying"* is an important hypnotic suggestion. No one wants to appear *"foolish,"* so that word is also important to remember. No one wants to mar their appearance, so the words *"nicotine stains"* are important. Annoying, foolish, and nicotine stains are *negative* words.

Now for some positive aspects of giving up cigarettes: sleep better, eliminate nausea and heartburn, have whiter teeth, have cleaner looking hands, eliminate throat irritation, eliminate smoker's cough, and, believe it or not, decrease tension. These are immediate benefits—a long range advantage: your LIFE!

Did you ever see a chain smoker who was relaxed? He appears to be a jittery person, puffing away on a cigarette. That's how you appear, too, everytime you light up. It is evident to everyone you have made nervousness a habit.

Do you *enjoy* smoking? Many smokers detest it. Do you? Remember the word *"detest."*

Countless persons have stopped smoking through self-hypnosis. In my own family I have an aunt who smoked two packs a day from age twenty-three until the age of fifty-one. One hypnosis session and she has never touched a cigarette again, and she is now sixty-five! And she didn't gain weight after stopping. There is no consistent evidence people gain weight after quitting the smoking habit.

Most subjects report they are able to stop smoking completely after four sessions of hypnosis. Now make your decision. Is it at least worth a try? Well, a try won't be good enough. *Determination* is what is needed. Determine yourself, here and now, to make a complete and final decision to quit smoking—not cut down, but quit altogether. And that means now. Determination will supply motive, and motive, as pointed out previously, is an important part of self-hypnosis therapy.

You can strengthen your determination by repeating to yourself daily why you want to give up smoking, and what it is doing to your health and appearance. It is a *poison* you are putting into your mouth, into your bloodstream, into your lungs, and into your heart.

Now let us deal with the *taste* of a cigarette.

Smoke in your mouth doesn't *taste* like a good steak, does it? It doesn't taste like sweet candy. It doesn't taste like that delicious dish served at your favorite restaurant. Ask yourself what it does taste like. Dry? Hot? Burning charcoal? Menthol? Foul? You will be suggesting to yourself that cigarette smoke tastes exactly like something you detest. What taste do you detest? What taste absolutely revolts you? Some of the most common comparisons are garlic, onions, spinach, cod-liver oil, gasoline, a melted aspirin, hot peppers, raw alcohol, or warm animal blood.

Giving Up Cigarettes

Take a sheet of paper and write down why you want to stop smoking. List what bad effects smoking is having on you and your health. Study what you have written. You are ready to begin:

1. The breathing exercise.
2. The candle-glow and afterimage exercise.
3. The auto-relaxation dialogue.
4. The dot-in-the-center-of-your-forehead concentration. Now tell yourself,

"You can control your mind, you can control your body. You can do anything you make up your mind to do. You have made a final decision to stop smoking cigarettes—now. You know what I say is the absolute truth and you know every time in the future the thought of a cigarette pops into your mind, the words *poison, annoying, foolish, nicotine stains, smoker's cough,* and *eventual death* will race through your mind.

"You will be happy and proud that you have determined to never smoke again. You know your friends and loved ones will admire you for this determination. And you are determined. Each and every time you put a cigarette to your lips, you will picture yourself placing a drop of poison on your tongue. Each and every time you experience the taste of smoke in your mouth, you will at the same instant experience the taste of (use the taste you detest most here) and you will detest that experience. Immediately, you will take the cigarette and break it in two, feeling proud and rewarded you have destroyed a killer.

"You really don't enjoy smoking, and you will never do it again, because it is a repulsive, unhealthy, costly habit. Anytime you wish to reinforce your determination to quit smoking, you will grip your left thumb with your right hand and instantly you will become as completely relaxed as you are now, and the thought of a cigarette will be repulsive to you, disgusting to you. Now you're going to do the things you want to do and you're going to do them confidently. One of the things you will want to do is to stop smoking completely, and you want to do it now! You will awaken on the count of three feeling refreshed, free of pain or body dis-

comfort, relaxed in every way. One . . . two
. . . getting brighter . . . three, awake!"

Repeat this session daily. Do not permit yourself to skip a day. Write your progress down on a calendar, looking forward to showing your progress chart to someone to impress them with your power of determination. After the fourth day, inject a new suggestion.

"I will never again even purchase a pack of cigarettes. Each time I am tempted to purchase cigarettes I will feel a terrible resentment at parting with my money for such a poison."

After the seventh day—a whole week without smoking, aren't you proud of yourself—add still another suggestion,

"Every day in every way, I'm getting better and better!"

And the truth is, you will!

You will have new respect for what you are capable of doing. That, in itself, is an important step on the road to mental health.

Chapter 10

DEVELOP YOUR SUCCESS MECHANISM

Now that you've had an introduction to self-hypnosis, and have had an opportunity to take a few practice swings at it, it is time for the regular season to begin. By the time you reach the final chapter of this book, you will be in the "world series" of discovering new things about yourself. You will have learned the laws of the mind and how to use these laws to your own advantage.

One of the important steps will be that you will learn how to change your self-image so it will automatically be a positive force in your work, in your social life, and in your health. It will become a brand new tool to be used to attain happiness and success.

You will have learned the true nature of your subconscious mind and how it can be programmed to release your hidden potential. You will also know what role your conscious mind plays in this process of releasing new and powerful energy. You will come to know by heart your own levels of thinking, and what is more important, how to control them. You will realize you have a success mechanism within yourself. Once awakened, it will be a positive personal force, enabling you to accomplish any goal. It will no longer be necessary to strain to attain these goals. That will be a part of your past.

You will have acquired the technique to change attitudes which, up until now, have made your walk through this life less comfortable than it might be. You will be able to release that great store of creative ideas dammed up by inhibitions. Your talents will no longer be imprisoned; your abilities will no longer be chained. You will have the exciting world of imagination at your disposal, anytime you choose to call upon it. You will experience a new awareness. You will know exactly how to control your own destiny with mathematical accuracy, charting your life in a new and rewarding direction.

Creativity

In this age of stress, we use our brain too much. It should only be used to gather information, make observations, set our goals, and form judgments. Too many people go beyond that, giving the conscious mind duties it wasn't meant for. The result is stress.

The dean of American psychologists, William James, once wrote, "When once a decision is reached and execution is the order of the day, dismiss absolutely all responsibility and care about the outcome. Unclamp, in a word, your intellectual and practical machinery, and let it run free; and the service it will do you will be twice as good. Give up the feeling of responsibility, let go your hold, resign the care of your destiny to higher powers, be genuinely indifferent as to what becomes of it all. It is but giving your private convulsive self a rest, and finding a greater SELF is there."

A greater self. Think about that for a moment.

A problem presents itself. What do we do? Usually we get a hunch or an inspiration. We have first thought about the problem consciously, become interested in it, interested in solving it. So we gather all the information we can on the subject. We think about it consciously, and thus intensify our urge and desire to solve the problem. But after we have defined the problem, we usually see in our imagination the desired end result. It's a hunch or an inspiration, and it didn't come from our *conscious mind*. Where then? From our unconscious mind, of course, because that is *its* function. Additional fretting, struggling, and worrying in our conscious mind does not help one iota. The truth is, worry only *hinders* the solution.

Charles Darwin, writing about an intuitional flash that came to him out of the blue, after torturous months of *conscious* thought about a

111

problem, said, "I can remember the very spot in the road, whilst in my carriage, when to my joy the solution *occurred* to me."

This was Darwin's *success mechanism* working, his own creativity blooming. Each and every one of us are creative, whether we be students, housewives, school teachers, garbage collectors, or bookkeepers. An inventor uses his creativity in his work. We may use our creativity in our everyday life. The mistake we make is employing *conscious* effort to solve a problem. This inhibits and jams the automatic creative mechanism.

When you go to the race track, the time to do your worrying and figuring is before post time. When the caller cries, "It is now post time!" your bet should be down. There is, in fact, nothing you can do about your bet after that. The decision has been made, and there is no use fretting about it. No *conscious* effort will do anything but get you up tight and produce stress.

As we have already mentioned, there are two separate divisions of the mind. The two, when used in unison, are a powerhouse.

The first division, the *conscious* mind, receives impulses from the outside world during our waking hours by means of the five senses. It can also *reject* impulses from the outside world. It can weigh and decide. The mature person weighs the impulses he receives throughout the day and decides what is important and what is unimportant. It is a logical and reasoning mind, and its most important job is to program the subconscious, or unconscious mind. It is the responsibility of the conscious mind to feed goals to the subconscious.

The *subconscious* mind records all the impulses

112

that happen in a lifetime, with the single provision that said impulse is carried into the subconscious mind with emotion. The purpose of the subconscious mind is to translate the impulse or picture into reality. For example, if someone looks you straight in the eye and with sincerity says, "I like you," it's translated into results right then. It makes you feel good. It is so powerful it can easily make you like someone else or cause you to take a positive attitude towards the entire day. It can be translated into more productive work on your job. Throughout your experience with hypnosis, you should remember the purpose of the subconscious mind is to translate a picture into practical reality.

The subconscious mind knows no bounds. You can think little or you can think big! You can build a canoe or a yacht or an oceanliner.

The subconscious mind does not have a choice as to the positiveness or the negativeness of an impulse. It only develops what is planted. And the subconscious mind is completely unaware of time. It can put anything off to the future, sometimes the distant future. You may retain an attitude for 20 years. You could have a poor self-image because your father told you at age seven you were "dumb like your Uncle Charlie."

The subconscious mind does not decide on the rightness or wrongness of an impulse. This is the function of our conscious mind, using a developed set of values.

One Idea At A Time
Opposing ideas cannot be held at one and the same time.

Many people try to hold opposing ideas simultaneously. But at any given moment you can consciously only be holding either the thought of succeeding or the thought of failing in accomplishing your personal goal. You cannot be thinking of both at the same time. It is this realization that gives you control over each individual thought you hold in your mind at any given moment. The individual thought has the power to set into action the principles of fulfilling your ambitions.

Once an idea is accepted by your subconscious mind, it remains until it is replaced by another idea. But the longer that original idea is held, the more it tends to become a fixed habit of thinking. This is how habits are formed. Both good and bad habits. First there is the thought and then the action. It must be understood that we have habits of thinking as well as habits of action. But the thought or idea was the first step in the conditioning. That fixed habit of thought that a person must have a drink or a cigarette or a tranquilizer before he can perform effectively is of course preposterous. But the idea is there—a fixed habit of thought. There will be opposition, however, to replacing it with a correct idea. No matter how fixed such habits of thought are in the subconscious mind—and no matter how long they have remained—they *can* be changed with self-hypnosis and positive repetition.

When dealing with the subconscious mind, the greater the conscious effort, the less the subconscious responds. This proves why willpower really doesn't work. If you have insomnia, you have certainly learned the harder you try to go to sleep, the more impossible it becomes. The rule is easy. When dealing with your subconscious mind, take it easy. As your faith in your own ability to manage your subconscious mind increases you learn to let it happen rather than try to force it to happen.

Now try this thought on for size: the one whose verdict counts most in your life is the person you see when you look in the mirror. Other people's opinions of you will change, but you have to live every moment of every day with your opinion of yourself. Have you cheated that person in the mirror? Have you been something less than honest with that person? That person will be with you until the day you die, you know, so best set things straight.

And that brings us to the subject of self-image. It relates to everything we do, say, and most of all what we consciously think. It influences our self-confidence in every situation.

Now that you have become receptive to self-hypnosis through the exercises in the previous chapters, let us try another technique. It is designed to build a new self-image, self-confidence, poise, and self-respect. Read the exercise aloud, *with conviction and feeling,* to convey the proper emotional message to your subconscious mind. After you have read it aloud two or three times, then say it to yourself, trying to remember as much of it as you can. It is all right if you find yourself substituting your own words. The core of the message is what is important, and the images that appear in your subconscious will be translated into positive actions.

Relax on a couch or bed in a safe, comfortable position.

Imagine that in the background you hear the sound of running water. The sound of flowing water has a very soothing effect on the human mind and nervous system. Actually hear the sound of running water. Listen to it, let it relax you.

Next, perform the breathing exercise.

Then the candle-glow staring. Close the eyes for ten seconds. Open them.

Now speak to your unconscious mind, telling it, with feeling,

"You will relax in response to certain words. These words are a relaxing stimulant, and from this moment on, each time you hear these words or think these words, your entire body will relax. The relaxation will be automatic, instantaneous, delightful.

"From this moment on, each time you hear or think the words *peaceful blue lake* you will instantly respond by relaxing both your mind and your entire body. Now you know that these words actually are words that will prepare you to relax, signal you to relax, free from worry or stress. The moment you form the thought after hearing or thinking the words *peaceful blue lake* you will right then and there allow your mind and body to relax. In a moment, I'll tell you when, I want you to take a deep breath in . . . hold it . . . and then I will say the words *peaceful blue lake*. When I do so, you will exhale, close your eyes, and you will feel a wonderful wave of relaxation, starting at the top of your head and floating right down to the tips of your toes. You will, at that instant, *let go* of all the tensions in your body and conscious mind. Ready now. . . .

"Take a deep breath . . . in . . . in . . . in. Hold it. *Peaceful blue lake.* Exhale, close your eyes and let go.

"Feel the wonderful wave of relaxation in response to these words, this signal. You feel better already, don't you? Now the next time you hear those words, you will relax ten times as much as you are right now.

"Take a deep breath . . . in . . . in . . . in. Hold it. *Peaceful blue lake.* Exhale, keep your eyes closed and let go.

"Now concentrate on your legs. Stiffen them, making your knees stiff and toes pulled back. Take a deep breath . . . in . . . in . . . in. Hold it. *Peaceful blue lake.* Exhale, let go, relax. Let your legs go limp.

"Now concentrate on your arms and stiffen them, elbows stiff, fingers extended, palms down. Take a deep breath . . . in . . . in . . . in. Hold it. *Peaceful blue lake.* Exhale, let go. Feel the muscles and nerves of the upper arms, elbow, lower arm, hands, fingers, go completely relaxed, loose, and comfortable.

"All your completely relaxed muscles simply will not work until you order them to do otherwise."

Now address yourself directly to your unconscious mind,

"Now you know what I say is the absolute truth. You now realize that having a true

117

self-image is the real secret to success. You now know that the self-image is the common denominator, the determining factor in every successful plan or project you will have from now on. From this moment on, you will find life satisfying. You now have a self-image that you are *proud* of. You now find yourself *acceptable* to you. You now have wholesome self-respect. You now have a self that you trust and believe in. You now have a self that you feel free to express creatively. You now have a self that corresponds to reality.

"You are now a whole person living effectively in a real world. You now know yourself, both your strengths and your weaknesses, and you are honest with yourself concerning both.

"Your self-image is now intact and secure. You now feel wonderfully good about yourself. You now feel supremely self-confident, you now feel free to be yourself and to express yourself to one or a hundred or a thousand people at a time, complete in the knowledge that you have within you vast untapped potentials.

"You were actually *created* with the inbuilt power to help yourself. You have no limitations except those you have imposed upon yourself. You now will create *positive* self-fulfilling phophecies. You will, from this moment on, treat yourself with self-respect. You now have a self-image that is only concerned with releasing your talents and potentials that you already have. You now know that there is, within your mind, a success mechanism, and you are determined to let it work for you effortlessly and easily. You now realize that you *deserve* to be successful, *deserve* to be happy.

"*You now love your neighbor and love yourself. You will no longer compare yourself with others. There is no one exactly like you and you are exactly like no one else, and you are proud of this. You are, yourself, unique in the universe—the entire universe.*

"From this moment on you will greet each stranger as a possible best friend. Anytime you wish to reinforce *all* these affirmations in your own mind, all you need do, and all you *will* do is say to yourself the words *peaceful blue lake* and instantly your mind will know that all these self-image thoughts are true and factual.

"Now awaken on the count of three. Feeling good and feeling confident. One . . . two . . . three! AWAKE!"

A tape recording (cassette) of this *Self-Image Hypnosis* exercise is available and may be obtained by writing to:

The Self-Discovery Institute Center
1888 Century Park East
Suite Ten
Century City
Los Angeles, California 90067

The *Self-Image* tape is one of the five-tape Self-Hypnosis course the Self-Discovery Institute Center endorses. I have been impressed with the effectiveness of the tapes. The tapes are especially skillful in the cure of smoking, insomnia, nervousness, and in inferiority complex. The entire

119

five-tape course costs $50.00.

Private self-hypnosis sessions (no groups) at the Center are available at $20.00 per visit. I investigated these private sessions and found them to be competent and adaptable to almost any personal problem.

Chapter 11

THINK AND GROW HEALTHY

When the magnitude of our body and its capacities is realized, we are awed by this beautifully constructed vehicle. We should resolve to give our body the care it so genuinely deserves. We are thankless and thoughtless stewards of an instrument that so marvelously and faithfully serves us. It is indeed fortunate the body survives much abuse. If our body is given adequate nutrition, proper exercise, and sufficient rest, coupled with constructive and loving care, it will last much longer than the commonly accepted three score and ten years.

Proof of this is the chicken heart that was kept alive in a jar for twenty-three years by Dr. Alexis Carrel. He carefully nurtured the chicken heart and eliminated the waste products of metabolism. Dr. Carrell has concluded the heart could live forever if this process were faithfully continued.

Proper care of the body can insure a long life. But it must be emphasized over and over again that the quality of the cells and the texture of the skin can be no better than the nutrition supplied them. It is for this reason the body must be given fresh fruits and vegetables. There is abundant vitality transmitted from these natural foods. While researching *ACUPUNCTURE AND YOUR HEALTH,* (Books For Better Living, $1.50), I was fascinated with the hundreds of years of Chinese research that has time and time again concluded that the balance of bodily health (the Chinese call it the Yin and Yang factors) is largely dependent on a diet of the foods nature supplies directly.

Above all we must resolve to keep active all the days of our lives. The body is built to move. It needs action. The physiological processes need the movement and massage of our muscles. The elimination of waste products from our bodies is aided by proper exercise.

But do not forget that a physical fitness program must be supplemented with positive thinking. Proper physical care can be cancelled out by a mind consumed with destructive thoughts. The mind holds a firm grasp over the body. In fact, it often holds the power of life and death.

Every thought or fear causes a physical reaction. Your mind affects your body. Worry causes

122

ulcers. Anger stimulates your adrenal glands. Anxiety and fear affect your heart, pulse rate, and blood pressure. Become aware of what you are thinking. Repetition of thoughts that have a *strong* emotional content reproduce the same bodily reaction over and over again. In order to eliminate chronic physical reactions, we must reach the subconscious mind and change the ideas responsible for the reaction.

Positive Expectations

What we imagine tends to become a reality. In other words, what we imagine becomes a self-fulfilling prophecy. What is expected tends to be realized. It does not matter if an image comes from something that happens in the external world or if the image is self-induced. The images formed from either source become the blueprint the subconscious mind uses to carry out the plan. Worry is a form of programming—an image of what you do *not* want. But the subconscious mind acts to fulfill the pictured situation. In the Bible, Job stated, "The things I have feared have come upon me."

An individual who suffers from anxiety is truly expecting, subconsciously, that something terrible is going to happen to him. On the other hand, what seems to be just plain good fortune in some people's lives is in reality positive mental expectancy—a strong belief they *deserve* to be successful.

We become what we think about. Our physical health is largely dependent upon our mental expectancy. Physicians recognize if a patient *expects* to remain sick, lame, paralyzed, helpless . . . even to die, the expected condition is often realized. Self-hypnosis can become the tool to remove negative attitudes and bring about a hopeful, positive expectancy.

Imagination is more powerful than knowledge when dealing with your own mind *or* the mind of another. Reason is easily overruled by imagination. Violent crimes committed as an act of jealousy are almost always prompted by an active imagination. Most of us feel superior to those who lose their savings to con men or blindly follow madmen like Hitler. Such people have allowed their imagination to overcome their reason. But we are often blind to our own superstitions, prejudices, and unfounded beliefs. Any idea accompanied by a strong emotion such as anger, love, or hatred usually cannot be modified by reason. Using self-hypnosis we can remove, alter, or amend old, negative ideas.

Every living person possesses the power for performance far above his present level of achievement. Yet, for the great majority of people, this power remains unused throughout life. Their store of inner strength is never unlocked, never utilized to make their bodies and minds—their whole lives—more productive and happier.

What you are really doing in your self-hypnosis sessions is saying to this power within, "I know you're there, and now I'm calling upon you to show yourself; go into the action I know you're capable of."

I Think, Therefore I Am

Think abundance, not limitation. The best way to begin to do that is by becoming more aware of the abundance manifested in nature and in the entire universe. Absolutely refuse, right here and now, to enclose yourself in a circle of limitation. Put yourself in that circle, and you will never step beyond its boundaries or even think of escaping. But realize, again right here and now, that you do have this power within you to break out of the circle. You want results. You no longer "desire" results. You now DEMAND them! And because you have this power within you, you *deserve* them.

You have a silent partner in life—your subconscious mind. You know it is there. You know how it works. You know it will take orders from you. Whatever project you give it, the subconscious will do everything in its power to materialize in your life the success of the plan you've programmed.

The success mechanism is always striving to successfully complete any assignment. Once given an idea, this success mechanism will carry an idea out to a conclusion in ways that often will seem astounding to you. Like the "smart" bomb used during the Vietnam conflict, your success mechanism will always guide your plan toward its goal. All you need be is the pilot. Keep your target on the television screen, and the success mechanism will hit target each and every time.

This wonderful success mechanism will never guide you to any goal higher than your own self-image. If you believed Daddy when he told you at age seven you are "dumb like your Uncle Charlie," (and a child certainly would—at that age a child's subconscious mind is programmed that Daddy and Mommy are always right) you will always think

125

of yourself as dumb. That is, until you remove that idea by replacing it with a positive, constructive idea. Keep that idea on center screen, repeating it every day under self-hypnosis, until the self-image accepts the new, positive idea as a fact.

A large sales organization has a salesman who earned $5,000 a year for his first four years with the company. They tried to elevate him and gave him a shot at their best territory. He ended up the year having earned $5,000. They transferred him to their poorest territory for the next year. Result—$5,000 income. The same thing happened the following year when they transferred him to an average sales quota territory. This man had a self-image that told him, day in and day out, he was a $5,000 a year man, nothing more, nothing less. It made no difference that his cost of living had gone up, that everyone around him needed more money to live on in these inflationary years. He pictured himself as a $5,000 a year man.

Why didn't he picture himself as a $10,000 or a $100,000 a year man? Perhaps, when he was starting his career, he sat down and figured out the bare minimum he needed to live. Then he asked himself if he was capable of earning that. He decided he was. He'd survive. The results could have been predicted the very first day he went to work for the company. Five thousand dollars each and every year of his life. The success mechanism will never guide you to any goal higher than your own self-image.

Since ninety percent of your creative power is in your subconscious mind, all you really have to do is impress it with your demand for success for whatever goal you seek.

What is my personal opinion of myself? What is my self-image?

Do you, like the $5,000 a year man, have a fixed negative image of yourself? You have always weighed 200 pounds and always will, no matter what you eat? You *are* a fat person.

In most cases, obesity and emotional maladjustment are related. The man or woman who eats compulsively is driven by an unconscious motivation to do so. There is a conflict, deep down. The first job is to uncover the cause of the compulsion.

Why do you overeat? When do you overeat? Do you eat compulsively when you're nervous? Nervous tension, an argument with a mate or a member of the family, a deadline at work, or any unusual pressure will cause certain persons to eat to excess, while others are driven to reach for a drink or cigarette. Consuming popcorn at the movies is a nervous habit. The more exciting the picture, the more popcorn sold.

Are you love-starved and lonely? Is food the only remaining consolation or pleasure you have left in life. Have you cut yourself off from emotional relationships, so that you receive no solace from another human being. Are you regressing back to your childhood and seeking the secret delights of a stolen cookie, a piece of birthday cake or candy? Do you sneak-eat? Do you reward yourself for a hard day by eating yourself into oblivion?

After you have pondered some of these questions about your eating patterns, we'll begin to attack the problem.

Give yourself the relaxing signal words.

Induce the hypnotic state by concentration on the white dot.

Admit to yourself that you have a problem.

Decide to do something about it *now*.

Remind yourself that you can do anything you make up your mind to do.

Tell yourself you will no longer consume food your body has no way to use. This is an abuse of your body and a waste of food.

Tell yourself all the reasons you would like to lose weight.

Memorize the foods you absolutely will not eat in the next seven days. Memorize the kinds of food you *will* eat. You will be guided by good nutrition, number of calories, and common sense. Decide what you are going to eat, how often you are going to eat, and how much you are going to eat. Give yourself the posthypnotic suggestion you will not deviate from your new diet, not even *want* to. Tell yourself that your mind is now in command, and temptation will be *easily* defeated.

Promise yourself in seven days you will begin to *admire* your new, slimmer appearance. Promise yourself that in fourteen days your body will feel healthier. You will feel free and proud of your progress. Promise yourself that in twenty-one days of a healthy, sensible diet, someone, somewhere, will compliment you, "My, how thin you're getting." When you receive this compliment, you will burst with pride. Your self-image is changing!

But most important of all! Promise yourself

128

that you'll be right back here at the same old stand tomorrow, at the same time, for your next five-minute self-hypnosis therapy.

When incorporated with all you have learned thus far in this book, *this program works!*

Chapter 12

CONQUER YOUR NUMBER ONE FEAR

Many fears the mind harbors can be traced back to a *fear of criticism*. This one, major fear can control your existence and wind its crippling, destructive way into every aspect of one's life.

How did this monster develop?

At birth, we begin an exciting journey into self-discovery. We explore, investigate, and experience many wonderful things. Watch when a baby discovers its fingers. He stares at them, not knowing what they are for. The baby crams them in his mouth and discovers he can manipulate those fingers. He moves them about in his mouth.

Next, he discovers the same fingers can be used to pick up things. That leads to the day when the baby learns to feed himself. He grabs a handful of food, aims for his mouth, and promptly hits his nose, eyes, or ears. But no mother would punish a baby for this, because she knows the child has to learn by making mistakes. In fact, she can hardly wait until Daddy comes home to show baby off. The two of them encourage the baby to try again.

Along comes the first birthday, the one when baby slaps the cake with both hands, and gets frosting all over himself. Daddy snaps a picture of the whole mess, and Mommy laughs. Again, no punishment when baby is falling down all over the house learning to walk. To the contrary, baby is praised for his efforts. Daddy holds his arms out and says, "C'mon, walk to daddy, try it again!"

The baby feels safe. He learns rapidly because he has *no fear of making a mistake*.

One day a child's all too brief period of learning without fear comes to a sudden halt. He made a mess, and this time, an adult's temper blows up; the child is scolded. He is told he is *bad!* At that moment the child's subconscious receives a terrible shock. Those raving words went deep into the feeling mind, and the next step is obvious. In a split second, the child's belief in itself begins to weaken. A new experience is recorded—rejection by another human being. In that split second the child learns the fear of criticism, and the poor kid begins to lose his true self.

The disaster of losing one's self begins with that first shock of criticism. When a child is criticized, he knows he is not being accepted for what he is; someone desires him to be something different than his natural self. The child feels his natural self must not be acceptable. The child stops being natural and begins the painful project of taking on a set of artificially conditioned responses. Years later, as an adult, that child may still be searching for that lost true self. At the same time, he may be afraid to find it, afraid to drop the behavior roles he has been conditioned to play in life. After all, didn't that adult, as a child, decide that his natural self was not acceptable?

We are all that baby. We all suffer from the fear of criticism. The difference is in the degree to which we suffer and the kind of situations that cause us to suffer. Some of us are afraid to express love and affection; some are afraid to express temper; some, both. Some of us are afraid to express *anything*.

Now let's get one point straight. No normal person enjoys being criticized. The fear of criticism resides in every human being on the face of the earth. It is a fear that can be overcome, put into perspective, and cut down to size. It was placed in our lives, and it can be removed. If it didn't happen to come from our parents, then it came from a teacher, or classmates. Whenever it occurred, we all made a promise to ourselves, naturally reasoning there must be some way to avoid criticism. We decided that whatever that way was, we were going to employ it. At that moment we stopped being free, stopped behaving spontaneously. Unfortunately, an enthusiasm for life was also lost.

Earlier, we also said you—yes, *you*—are a very special, unique individual. There's not another one exactly like you.

But have you stopped expressing that individual, stopped being that person you really are? Have you lost your enthusiasm for life? Better

132

get it back. It's the only life you have. Are you nursing this loss by hiding your true feelings from the people around you? If you have, you have learned a painful lesson in inhibition. You learned to keep the real you locked up inside of you like a prisoner in solitary confinement. You have altered your true personality, only expressing what others expect of you. You choose to play roles, roles you cannot be criticized for, on the stage of life.

Was this good reasoning?

Of course not.

But the subconscious mind cannot reason, remember? These reactions were nothing but conditioned responses in your subconscious mind, forming a pattern (a ridiculous one at that!) that became a part of your self-image.

Are You A Perfectionist?

What happened? Did you decide to make yourself perfect? Do you have the "I can, I will, I must!" syndrome? Psychiatrists might call you an over-achiever. Did you make unreasonable demands on yourself until you became perfect? Did you say to yourself as a child, if I could just achieve perfection, nobody could criticize me? I'm sure you can see that's nonsense, now.

Ever watch a fly in a bottle? The fly looks pretty desperate to get out, and full of fear he won't. Is that you? Are you trying to come out in the open and do what comes naturally?

The opposite reaction to criticism is the under-achiever. This person says to himself, "I just won't try. If I don't try, I can't be criticized. So, I'm a loser. I never could do anything right.

Mommy and Daddy were always right, weren't they? I never will. Now if I can just make myself satisfied watching other people doing things I wish I had the nerve to do, I'll be perfectly safe from criticism. Right?"

Wrong.

Those are the two opposite extremes, and the odds are good you don't fall entirely in either camp.

Most of us are a complicated combination of an over-achiever and an under-achiever. Maybe we're good at our work, but miserable failures in our social life. Or vice versa.

Fear of making a mistake is the motivation in either case.

Fear of making decisions again relates to a fear of criticism. But realize, if you're going to be good and successful at anything you have got to make mistakes while learning. The one mistake you don't want to make is to let the fear of criticism create the fear of making a mistake, which in turn causes inhibitions, surfacing as other fears.

The under-achiever is constantly *comparing* himself with others. It is a hangup the under-achiever may not even recognize, frustrating as it may be. All the under-achiever is saying to his subconscious mind is he is unhappy with his own accomplishments. We tend to overlook our good points and compare what we haven't done to something someone else has done. To put it another way, don't we take our good qualities for granted, and dwell on our so-called failures? Wouldn't it be healthier to pat ourselves on the back for what we have accomplished? Remember, there isn't anyone in this entire world who is good at everything. If you decide here and now to treat both yourself and others with respect, then your first step is to stop comparing.

Are You A Role Player?

The over-achiever, on the other hand, sees himself as an actor in life, playing one role after another—lover, banker, the life of the party, salesman, psychologist, father of the year, organizer. You name it, he plays it. And his act is good. But inside he feels terribly empty. Why? Many people believe his act and envy him.

The trouble is this poor soul is certain no one could like the real person behind the masks. He spends his life keeping that part hidden. And so he play all these roles: one of the boys with the men, a lady's man with "broads." That's what he calls women when he's with the boys; to their face, it's "darling." He's a swinger at the Saturday night party, and a "holy Joe" Sunday morning on the church steps. Never himself, he acts the part that will make him acceptable to others. This person is so afraid of criticism, he will do anything to gain acceptance from other people.

He worships what other people think, and that's a lonely way to go.

Don't be either of these opposites or someone in between. Treat yourself with real creative self-respect. If you get up at five in the morning to clean the house because you're expecting the cleaning lady at eight, you're a perfectionist. You're playing an unnatural (and foolish) role, trying to impress the housekeeper. You would be amazed at how little the cleaning woman, or anyone else, for that matter, is concerned about you.

135

That woman is too busy being concerned about herself.

Try to be perfect, and you almost always guarantee failure. The perfectionist is a frightened, competitive person who feels he must always win. He is seeking security which to the perfectionist is being above criticism. He is a fault-finder. Nothing anyone else does is ever good enough for him. I can see women standing up all over the country shouting, "That's my husband!" What the perfectionist is usually doing is belittling others to make himself look better. He is reinforcing his own superiority. He has an urge to look good at the expense of someone else. It's as simple as that. He is a deeply fearful person, who protects himself by attacking others.

Now let's make a conscious decision: No more criticism. From now on you are going to treat yourself with self-respect. Forgive yourself for past mistakes. Stop criticizing yourself.

Become A New Person

Begin with the self-relaxation procedure. First step, breathing exercise, then candle-glow, then eyes closed, count one-to-ten backwards, relaxing a separate part of the body on each count. Hear running water in background, or have soft music playing.

Concentrate on the white dot in center of forehead.

Actually feel the sensation of your mind drifting out towards that dot.

Say to yourself:

"You are now going to recite the alphabet, just as you learned it in grade school. As a

136

matter of fact, you will *recall* the classroom where you learned the alphabet, recall reciting it as a child. You will actually see again that scene, that classroom, that teacher. As you recite the alphabet, and when you get to the letter '*J*' the picture of that classroom and everything about it will disappear from your mind, and you will experience a tingling, pleasant and light feeling in your left hand. Now as you say the letter '*L*' you will be fully concentrating on your left hand, picturing it completely relaxed, . . . a tingling sensation . . . in your hand . . . it is limp, heavy, relaxed, a pleasant feeling.

"As you reach the letter '*Q*' your hand is tingling, and the tingle is becoming stronger . . . stronger and stronger. As you reach the letter '*V*' your whole hand is tingling . . . pleasant and tingling! Harmless little needles and pins prodding your left hand. As you say the letter '*X*' you will *know* you are now in a state of self-hypnosis because your hand *is* tingling, and because you *are* in a state of hypnosis you are ready to give yourself beneficial posthypnotic suggestions. As you say the letter '*Z*' the sensation in your hand will go away instantly, and it will return to normal.

"You have now recited the entire alphabet, and every muscle and nerve in your entire body is relaxed. You now have proof that you have reached a state of hypnosis, and you now have proof that your subconscious mind is ready to receive constructive instructions.

"*From this moment on, each and every*

time you comb your hair, that combing of the hair will be the symbol to remind you that you are the greatest of all God's creatures. You now recognize the harmful effects of the fear of criticism. You now rise above those fears. To recognize the cause of a fear is to rob it of its mysterious qualities. You have now won half the battle. YOU NOW KNOW THE ENEMY.

"*Each time you comb your hair* a wonderful, thrilling release will occur within you in your emotions, thinking and your entire physical body. *Each time you comb your hair* you will feel *free!* Each time you comb your hair, it will be a signal to realize that every mistake you ever made in your life was part of the learning process, and the more mistakes you made, the more you learned about life and yourself.

"Each time you comb your hair you will *instantly* forgive yourself for each and every mistake you have ever made in your life. Each time you comb your hair, this will be the key to remind yourself that you are a unique individual. You will accept yourself as being different from every other human being on this earth. Each time you comb your hair, you will know that from now on you need only compete against your own accomplishments.

"*Each time you comb your hair,* this will be the key to remind you that you are enthusiastic about yourself, you now will thrill to the excitement of your own personal self, your own personal goals. You will know that

138

you now have a positive attitude, that you will achieve whatever goal you decide on. Each time you comb your hair, this will be the key to remind you that *YOU CAN DO ANYTHING YOU MAKE UP YOUR MIND TO DO*.

"Each time you comb your hair, this will be the key to remind you that your self-respect is now programmed to grow and grow, and that it will indeed grow . . . each time you comb your hair.

"Each time you comb your hair, this will be the key to remind you that the past is over and done with. You now tear out the yoke of past guilts. You now accept yourself as a human being, no more and no less. As a human being, you are the finest of all God's creatures. Each time you comb your hair, this will be the key to remind you that from this day on you will use the flow of words spoken solidly in your mind to describe all the wonderful, positive, constructive things about you.

"Each time you comb your hair, this will be the key to remind you that you now will make withdrawals of SELF-RESPECT from your subconscious mind, and that your subconscious mind has a TREMENDOUS store of self-respect for you, just waiting to be tapped.

"*Each time you comb your hair, this will be the key to remind you that the past is gone! Over! That you are you, and you like you, accept you, and you are above the need of false fears. Each time you comb your hair, this*

will be the key to remind you to automatical-
ly REJECT even the thought of past fears.
It will be impossible for you to even remem-
ber them. They are part of the past, were
destructive to the you that is you, and the
past is over with, gone!

"You now accept your own good thoughts
about yourself. You now love yourself . . .
and love your neighbor as yourself. You do
not compare yourself to anyone because you
now realize that you are unique, and every
other human being is unique, there are no
two alike, and there shouldn't be.

"All this self-respect, all this appreciation of the you that is you, all this creative,
positive, self-rewarding, self-accepting thinking will actually soar and surge through your
mind, through your body, through your entire being! . . . *every time you comb your
hair.*

"Now relax . . . just relax . . . as you go
even deeper . . . and deeper . . . and deeper
into the state of hypnosis. Concentrate on
relaxing the nerves about your eyes. Relax
the muscles about your eyes. The moment you
form the thought of relaxation in your own
mind, allow your eyes to relax and respond
to it. Now take a deep breath in . . . in . . . in.
Hold it. Exhale and relax ALL the muscles
about your eyes, as you go deeper . . . and
deeper . . . and deeper into the wonderful
state of hypnosis.

"Each time you comb your hair this will be
the key, the signal to remind you that you
will reject, disregard, shut out, spurn, omit,

strike off, cancel, eliminate, ban, eradicate, refuse, discard, discharge any negative thoughts of inferiority, lack of confidence or self-recrimination that may have visited your mind in the past and this will happen automatically . . . every time you comb your hair.

"Now actually FEEL! the entire length and breadth of your tongue relaxing . . . going loose . . . limp . . . and as it does, this feeling of limp calm spreads over your entire body—throat, chest, arms, legs, back.

"NOW YOU KNOW WHAT I SAY IS THE ABSOLUTE TRUTH. THE PAST IS GONE AND YOU ARE HERE. UNJUSTI- FIED FEARS OF THE PAST ARE GONE AND YOU ARE HERE. YOU ARE HERE IN THE PRESENT AND YOU ARE UNIQUE.

"You are proud of the you that is here. You are satisfied with the you that is here. You now see the absolute individual that is you. For the sake of your sanity and happiness, you will only react to reality of the here and now and the future. For the sake of your success mechanism and your tranquility, you will only react to what happens now and in the future, not to the past, for the past is gone, over. It is unfair, unjust and down- right foolish to judge yourself according to the past, for the past is gone, over.

"You are a new person. Your trip through life from now on will be as a whole person, living life completely, effectively, free of the past, free of criticism, free of past fears that you now know are unreal.

"You now know that you need not desire good fortune to overcome any unjustified fear, for you now know that you yourself are good fortune, and know that you have the power within you to travel the road of the future strong and content with yourself. You now know that unjustified fears of the past were *sick emotions* and you now know that whenever you are again confronted with this sick emotion your new found self-confidence will be your unfaltering partner, enabling you to bypass that sick emotion automatically, that through instant relaxation you will continue on the main road with your healthy, happy, strong *new self*.

"The past is gone, over, and in the future you are going to think with your wonderful mind and not the emotional intoxication of the fears you have suffered in the past. You now know the emotional intoxication of those fears dissipated your mental energy, and you will no longer permit that to happen to you because you like you. It will be almost impossible for you to even remember those, fears, let alone honor them, for they deserve no honor . . . they were not reality to begin with and you now know you will deal only with the reality. The past is dead and gone.

"THE FUTURE IS YET UNBORN.

"You will now approach each situation, not as a repeat of something out of your past, but as a possible new and wonderful experience, one that your new self can easily handle with the ease of the self-relaxation you now know you're capable of.

"Expect this relaxation to happen. Desire it to happen . . . and watch it happen. And as you do you will automatically become aware of your own mind relaxing, become aware of your own feeling of peace, contentment and well-being, free from fear or anxiety.

"Your breathing is now even and steady . . . even and steady . . . even and steady as you go deeper . . . and deeper . . . and deeper into the wonderful relaxation of the hypnotic state. Deeper . . . deeper . . . deeper down into the soft, velvety darkness.

"*Feel* that deep sense of peace with yourself.

"*Feel* that deep sense of harmony and tranquility. Peace . . . that surpasses all human understanding. You can actually *feel* your own marvelous brain relaxing . . . relaxing . . . relaxing . . . and as you do, you can actually see the unrealistic fears that visited you in the past drifting harmlessly downstream, leaving your life, evacuating your subconscious mind, leaving it free and happy, relieved of all past tensions and anxieties. They are gone, never to return, and you are happy about this. You can actually *see* yourself waving happily *goodbye* to them. You are taking a well deserved vacation from all the cares of the past. You are taking this vacation within your own mind and the feeling is grand!

"Anytime you wish to reinforce the posthypnotic suggestions you have given yourself in this session, all you need do . . . and will automatically do . . . is say the words MY

143

NEW SELF silently and you will instantly know that you are issuing a command to your subconscious mind to relax and to remember and to repeat every word of this session, programming it again and again onto its subconscious mind screen, where that command will be translated and obeyed, all in an instant.

"You will know that you are commanding your subconscious mind to send your past fears drifting downstream . . . going . . . going . . . gone out of your sight, never to return.

"When you silently say the words MY NEW SELF to yourself instantly your subconscious mind will flash every word of this session out for your conscious mind to grasp. You will believe these words and act upon them immediately, feeling confident, delightfully free of past fears and anxieties. You will feel superbly calm and relaxed. This reaction will be as automatic as the reactions you now know you will have *every time you comb your hair*.

'I want you to awaken now on the count of three, refreshed, relaxed, free from fear or body discomfort, normal in every way.

"One . . . getting brighter.

"Two . . . bright, bright!

"Three . . . open your eyes . . . awake . . . awake!"

A tape recording of this self-hypnosis therapy session can also be obtained from the Self-Discovery Institute Center, mentioned in Chapter 10.

Chapter 13

ANSWERING YOUR QUESTIONS

QUESTION:
I have now read and practiced the self-hypnosis techniques, and I find them very relaxing. But are these sessions adaptable to my own problems?
ANSWER:
What you have been taught to do here is *employ* the tremendous power of your own mind for whatever self-improvement goal you seek. Now that you have mastered the method of self-hypnosis, you are equipped and ready to give yourself specific instructions.

QUESTION:
While reading the self-hypnosis practice sessions, I actually felt myself going deeper . . . and deeper as suggested. Does this mean I'm weak-willed?

ANSWER:

No, it means just the opposite. The more intelligent and imaginative you are, the easier it is to slip into the hypnotic state.

QUESTION:

What about exhaustion? Can I boost my energy level through self-hypnosis? I seem to get very tired every afternoon, and if I don't take a good long nap I'm through for the day.

ANSWER:

Try the relaxation that self-hypnosis offers when you get tired in midafternoon. Give yourself the posthypnotic suggestion that on the count of three you will awaken refreshed and feeling as though you just had a nice two-hour nap. It might be smart to get a physical checkup as well. If your fatigue is mental, self-hypnosis can help. If it's physical, your doctor is your best bet.

QUESTION:

My problem is that I always seem to be nervous and irritable. It's like I'm in high gear. What suggestions can I give myself to relieve this tension?

ANSWER:

Remind yourself that God did indeed give you a sense of humor. Find the humor in each worrisome situation. Convince yourself, during the self-hypnosis session, that worry is a symptom of insecurity, evidence that you lack self-confidence. You *want* to attain self-confidence . . . and shall achieve it! Indulging in negative thinking is ignorant, and you are not ignorant. Tell yourself you

146

like yourself. See to it you enjoy the gift of laughter each day. Even your own nervousness has a comedic quality. Don't take yourself so seriously. Laugh at yourself.

Tell yourself that now that your mind is relaxed, you are free of any unpleasantness which makes you nervous. Make a promise (because you *like* yourself) you will devote five minutes of every day to your self-hypnosis relaxation therapy. To insure yourself against upset, give yourself the posthypnotic suggestion that all you need do . . . and all you will do . . . is grasp your left thumb with your right hand. This will be the signal . . . *the key* for you to relax your mind . . . your body. After that it will be impossible for you to become nervous over a situation. You will realize how temporary and insignificant it is in the overall picture of your life.

QUESTION:

That's all well and good, but who has time to think all those thoughts, helpful as they may be. What if some fear comes over me that sets my nerves on a rampage, my hands trembling. It would be swell if the feeling would pass. But my mind lingers on it, and ruins the rest of the day. More often than not, it keeps me awake that night, too. Is there anything I can do, or say to myself in an instant that will redirect my thoughts?

ANSWER:

Yes. Many people use the thumb-grabbing technique, but others need some object outside themselves to grab on to. I've found that a brilliant metal object makes an excellent point of concentration. One unique aid has been developed by a company in New York, which has sold over 100,000 of these hypnotic aids.

After the aid has been used several times during the hypnotic session, the person carries the aid with him in his pocket or purse. Because of the hypnotic suggestion, just touching the aid, during a moment of panic, will automatically create relaxation, remove fears, etc.

I realized how important a friend in the pocket aid is when I talked with an entertainer who does uncanny impressions of well-known people. I asked him how he was able to switch from one personality to another in an instant, sometimes in mid-sentence. He replied, "I use self-hypnosis. I have programmed myself to actually *become* a different character each time I touch that character's name on a metal plate in my pocket. What the audience doesn't notice is how I keep putting my hands in different pockets. That's my secret. I simply touch Jimmy Cagney, and in a split second I see and hear him, and through training, become him. The same is true with Jack Benny, Kirk Douglas, President Nixon, you name it. I carry a larger plate for John Wayne. Any impersonator will tell you he's the toughest image to make come through. I'll tell you another secret.

"After a performance in Vegas or New York, I go back to my hotel room pretty charged up, can't sleep. I'm still picturing myself as Cagney or Jimmy Stewart or whoever. So I have another metal plate—and it's nobody. I shine the night light on it, concentrate on the reflected gleam, and because I have given myself a posthypnotic suggestion, I'm asleep in about two minutes.

Nuts, eh?" No, not nuts. The brain can only concentrate on one thought at a time, remember? And that's the answer.

These self-hypnosis aids can be ordered by sending $4.95 along with your name and address to: Kaybar Associates, P.O. Box 221, Bellerose, New York 11426. Attention: Friend-In-The-Pocket Aids.

QUESTION:

I have a morbid fear of failure. Can self-hypnosis help me to think my way to success?

ANSWER:

Let me tell you about a fellow who must be one of America's most famous failures. In 1832 he failed in business. He did it again in 1833. Between 1834 and 1856 he failed in political bids in eight different elections! In 1860 he was elected to President of the United States. His name was Abraham Lincoln. He knew what he was after. He didn't give up. It's time to re-evaluate your own self-image. Learn to believe you deserve success through self-hypnosis therapy.

QUESTION:

My problem is depression. In a few minutes I can swing from being ecstatic to a miserable depression.

ANSWER:

Your first step is to find out why this happens. This can be done through autoanalysis. Ask yourself if you are too sensitive to criticism. Are you living in the past, using those old values to judge yourself? Do you get irritable when you are tired? Are you too shy? Are you playing the childish act of seeking sympathy from your family and friends? Are you suspicious of people? Is the reason behind your depression resentment or disillusionment at having been hurt by someone you love or once loved? Are you pessimistic about your future? Do you consider yourself the direct target of misfortune and bad luck?

Well, stop kidding yourself. It's time to *like* yourself. Give yourself the benefit of the doubt. You have put yourself on trial and unfairly. Divert your mind, right here and now, from yourself. Tell yourself, after the self-hypnosis relaxation exercise,

"You are going to forget the misfortunes of the past. The past is dead and gone. You are going to begin to live today and you are going to search out the many enjoyments life has to offer. You are going to do the things you want to do. You are going to picture your life as a delicious meal on a plate in front of you, and you are going to salt and pepper it exactly to your taste. And because life tastes good, it will give you a feeling of well-being.

"What used to annoy you will, from this moment forward, be amusing. Because you are smarter now, because you know yourself better now, each day you will think how fortunate you are to be alive.

"You will picture each day as a dollar bill removed from your savings account. Certainly you would not throw a dollar bill in the gutter. Just as certainly, you will not throw days of your life away. Each day is to be cherished. You will be grateful and happy for this day. Isn't it wonderful you can do anything you make up your mind to do? You will no longer think about the pros and cons of what you do, or whether you can do it.

"Win or lose, you will enjoy whatever you happen to be doing at the moment. Win or lose, you will savor the moment. Winning or losing is not important because you now *like yourself* in defeat as well as victory. You didn't stop rooting for your high school football team after a defeat, did you? And you're not going to stop rooting for yourself after some silly one day, one week, or one month defeat either. You are you. God loves you, and you love yourself. You absolutely refuse to suffer any longer."

Suggest to yourself that this tremendous feeling of happiness will come over your entire being each and every time you . . . (now you make up the posthypnotic suggestion). Shall it be grasping your left thumb with your right hand? Or thinking of a word or set of words? Or perhaps the memory of a face of someone who once paid you a compliment that affected you very favorably? Whatever technique you decide upon, tell yourself that you will react instantly with happiness, pride, and a smile. Watch it happen!

QUESTION:
I have a pain that bothers me. Can I overcome this discomfort through self-hypnosis?
ANSWER:
In all fairness to yourself, please don't try. See

your medical doctor and find out the cause of the pain. It may be nature's signal of trouble. Such a signal should not be ignored or hypnotized away.

QUESTION:
I am pregnant. Would you suggest childbirth under hypnosis?
ANSWER:
Childbirth under hypnosis is being researched with promising results. Aside from the use of hypno-anesthesia to induce painless childbirth, hypnosis has been used to develop a relaxed attitude in the expectant mother and to overcome postpartum depression. But, seek and follow the advice of your personal physician in this area.

QUESTION:
My husband is a "bim-bam-thank-you-ma'am" type of lover, and it is driving me insane with frustration. How can self-hypnosis help me with this problem?
ANSWER:
Get hubby to read this book, particularly Chapter 8. It might just show him he is capable of self-control and a tenderness he never knew he possessed. He'll learn that not only is he unique, but you are too. It will free him from sexual guilts which make him want to get the "shameful act" over with fast, before God and the world knows what he's been doing. It might just show him how silly this negative thought is. He controls his mind, and his mind controls his penis. This knowledge applies to both problems

of impotence and rapid ejaculation. If he learns to like himself and to forgive himself for his past deeds, he will not want to deprive himself of the joy that mutual sexual satisfaction can afford his ego.

QUESTION:

I am a student. When I'm about to take an examination I get so nervous I can't remember anything. I note that in one of your conditioning sessions, you give the posthypnotic suggestion that every word from the session will be remembered exactly. Can self-hypnosis really improve my memory?

ANSWER:

No ifs, ands or buts about it. Relaxation is the answer. In his book, *Helping Yourself With Self-Hypnosis,* Frank S. Caprio, M.D., tells of screen star Linda Darnell's dilemma in learning every line of her lead role in the play *Late Love* which was about to open. A doctor who practiced hypnosis "placed her in such a state of relaxation and receptivity" she was able to learn the lines in only two sessions. Many actors employ hypnotism to memorize page after page of scripts.

In my work I have been associated with film people who make a practice of picking up their scripts at the studio and then drive directly to their hypnotist. They are completely relaxed and absorb a posthypnotic suggestion before they sit down to memorize their lines. You can do the same thing with your studies. Complete relaxation is the answer. Add self-confidence, and eliminate negative suggestion, and go to your examination expecting success.

QUESTION:

My mother was a nervous person, and I guess that's why I'm so nervous. Can self-hypnosis do anything about inherited traits.

ANSWER:

It doesn't have to. Personality traits are *not* inherited. What has probably happened (unless both you and your mother have physical nervous disorders) is that you are *imitating* your mother. As children we see our parents as giants. They know everything, have everything, and do everything we are told we're too young to do. We can't wait for the day when we can be like them —have a car, get married, buy a home, raise children and make up the rules and regulations.

The trouble is your subconscious mind can't reason, so it imitates the bad (your mother's nervous habit) as well as the good. Your mom could have been hypnotized out of her nervousness, and so can you. Remember you are unique, not like anyone else, not like your mother or your father. Do not compare yourself to anyone. Your own personality traits were learned and acquired. Now is the time to unlearn the ones you don't admire.

A Self-Hypnosis Miracle

Before we close, and you begin reviewing and practicing the self-hypnosis exercises outlined in this book, I'd like to cite one more case history to help you in your determination to continue with your self-hypnosis sessions, until you have solved each and every one of your problems.

Kathy is an attractive housewife in her mid-thirties. She is the mother of four fine children. She is popular, always wearing a big smile, and her husband is proud of her, indeed. But Kathy had one problem. It all surfaced after she had been married for ten years. It came upon her in a split instant. Here's how:

Kathy and her husband had planned a family European vacation for a long time. When the time came, they boarded a plane and flew to Paris. Kathy enjoyed the flight, the food aboard the plane, even the movie. On their second day in Paris, while the children were out sightseeing, Kathy and her husband visited the Arc de Triomphe. They rode the elevator right to the top where they could look out over the entire city. For those who haven't been there, the railing around the seemingly sky-high top level is ridiculously low. But Kathy was unafraid, looking straight down over the edge, until she saw two small boys do the same thing.

Kathy's head went into a spin. She began to tremble, became violently ill, and almost passed out.

And she didn't know why.

From that moment, the seed grew.

When they returned to their home in California, the cliff they lived on seemed ten times as high to Kathy. She refused to go out near the cliff edge —and yet it had been she who had planted the beautiful flowers out there before her European trip. She couldn't even get up on a ladder anymore. Her legs would tremble, and her head would spin in dizziness. Where did the fear come from? What had caused it?

The couple moved out of their cliff-side home.

Kathy avoided standing at the top of stairs and looking down—she avoided standing at the top of *anything* and looking down. She became nervous, irritable, having lost a certain self-confidence she had always thought was a complete and whole part of her. The fear became worse. She began to shut herself in at home where it was safe. Even when a close relative died in the east, Kathy refused to consider taking a plane and risked missing the funeral by going on a train instead. Even then, she had a difficult moment standing at the top of the train stairs, looking down just five or six feet.

It was a year and a half after the Paris trip before Kathy's doctor-hypnotist suggested hypnotic regression. Here is the answer that came out of the very first session.

Kathy, the hypnotist learned, had grown up in Chicago. She spent the first ten years of her life in a three-story tenement. Her mother worked as a seamstress, and her father was employed in the steel mills. After school each day Kathy was alone on the top floor until her mother came home around six.

One day Kathy was standing at the stairway railing on the top floor, looking down. In her hand was a transformer battery from a set of electric trains that belonged to her older brother, who was out delivering newspapers. Two floors below, a small neighbor boy appeared in the hallway. Kathy yelled something to him, and at that instant dropped the heavy transformer battery. It hit the little boy on the top of his head, cutting open his scalp. It bled, and Kathy screamed. The boy screamed.

Kathy ran down the two flights of stairs, looked at the screaming boy, the bloody head, and promptly ran back upstairs, crying hysterically. She went to a closet, got her older brother's pair of binoculars, and ran back downstairs. She offered the seemingly expensive binoculars to the boy if only he wouldn't tell his mother what a terrible thing she had done. She felt she would be unacceptable in that entire three-story house from then on, if the boy told his mother. Her mother came home. The boy's mother came upstairs. Kathy hid in the bedroom.

But no big deal was made out of it, except in Kathy's mind. The boy wasn't seriously injured. Her mother simply said, "You must be more careful not to hurt people, Kathy." And that was that.

Until twenty years later.

The subconscious mind does not forget. When Kathy saw those two boys leaning over the railing atop the famous French monument, the picture out of her childhood was finally *translated* by her subconscious mind. And without reasoning. The seed never died, it grew! The boys, leaning over and looking down, became little Kathy looking down from her third story railing in Chicago. There was blood! And screaming! And she was guilty!

The interesting thing about this true story is that Kathy never even gave this incident another thought during her years of growing up, becoming a wife and then a mother of four small children of her own. But the incident was there, always there, hiding in the background, just as she had hidden in her bedroom.

It took six hypnotic sessions for Kathy to forgive herself for all that blood, all that screaming. The hypnotist replaced that buried guilt with the idea of how beautiful it must be to look down at the earth from an astronaut's spacecraft and other positive thoughts. He gave Kathy the post-hypnotic suggestion she would want to go out to the local airport and listen to the sounds of the airport terminal, the sounds of planes overhead, and these would be pleasant sounds. He described the beauty of the symmetrical design of a stairway, how it has served man.

He pointed out the comical aspects of her childhood experience, having the little boy look up and shout, "That was a pretty good shot. Now can you part my hair on the left side instead of in the middle?"

He gave her the suggestion of the boy's mother coming upstairs and telling her mother, "Thank Kathy for me, will you? I've been trying to keep little Martin out of that hallway for months. He doesn't play out there in that dark hallway anymore, and I have Kathy to thank for it."

Through self-hypnosis, Kathy was able to unlock the secrets of her past and gained total self-acceptance of herself. She overcame her fear of height and resumed her normal life-style.

Now it is time to think about all you have read here. You are going to afford yourself the benefits of a five-minute self-hypnosis session each and every day from now on. This book promises you will discover a new you. *Today* is the first day of the rest of your life. You *can* control your mind, and you *can* control your body.

158